THE CLASSICS OF GOLF

Edition of

THE MYSTERY OF GOLF

by

Arnold Haultain

Foreword by Herbert Warren Wind
Afterword by John Updike

Foreword

It is generally agreed, I think, that golf has the finest literature of any game. It is also generally agreed that the principal reason for this is that golf is the only game played on natural terrain or on land shaped to resemble the terrain of the great Scottish links- land courses. This gives golf a whole different dimension than such games as tennis, football, hockey, basketball, soccer and many others that are played on flat courts or fields that must con- form to fairly exact specifications. Then, too, golf is played on a much larger tract of land than any other game—one that has room enough for eighteen separate holes. This makes it possible on courses of championship quality for each of the holes to develop its own distinct personality and to im- pose on the golfer special challenges because of its length, its contours, and the placement of the hazards that pa- trol its fairway and protect its green.

Golf is a very exacting game. The golfer has to learn to play a wide assortment of shots. Through mistakes in judgment or execution, he frequently throws away the chance of posting the best score of his life on a course he admires enormously. Say it is the Old Course at St. Andrews. After playing the first fifteen holes like a Jones or a Nicklaus, more often than not, because of the inevitable pressure that has accumulated, he will become entangled with the Principal's Nose on the sixteenth, with either the Road bunker or the road itself on the seventeenth, and with that confounded Valley of Sin on the eighteenth. Gone from his swing is that lazy Jonesian rhythm and that awesome Nicklausian power. The man who totters off the last green looks as if he had decided never to play the game again.

The nature of golf changes with the wind and weather, to be sure, and also with the kind of match the golfer is engaged in. Is he playing a singles at

*match play or medal play? They are
entirely different propositions psycho-
logically. Is he involved with a partner
in a foursomes match or a four-ball
match? There is quite a bit of difference between the two. If he is playing at
Muirfield, the home of the Honourable
Company of Edinburgh Golfers,
chances are that he will be playing a
foursomes, that form of golf in which
two partners play alternate shots and
drive from alternate tees. If he is playing at the National Golf Links of
America, more than likely he will not
be playing a foursomes but a four-ball
match, that form of golf in which each
partner plays his own ball just as he
does in a singles, and the lower score
registered by one of the partners on
each hole is the one that counts. The
Scots and the English prefer foursomes. Americans usually prefer the
four-ball match. You can take it a step
further, as is now common in the bi-
ennial Ryder Cup Matches in which
some of the members of each team are*

selected to play in the foursomes and four-ball matches as well as in the singles.

Will a player's individual excellence in a foursomes that was lost have a good or bad effect on his play in the singles? It is hard to know, because a large number of varied forces are always at work in golf, the only outdoor game in which a player is faced with hitting a stationary ball from a stationary position. It is a trying task even for an athlete with exceptional coordination to generate his own power from a stationary stance and still control the timing of his shot so that the ball flies in the right direction. Since it takes anywhere from two hours to five and a half hours to play a competitive round, what a burden is the mixed bag of pressure, tactical plans, true and bogus sportsmanship, psychological ease, mute terror, superstition, revisions of tactical plans, changes in the key movements of his swing, total acceptance of the world, and second thoughts about his new putter that the golfer carries around for such a considerable period of time. If anything, golf gives a golfer too much time to think about things.

Many men have tried to analyze why golf, despite the terrific punishment it inflicts on its faithful adherents, is such a fascinating game. Why is it that the Scot, who only moments before has hurled his clubs into the North Sea, dives into the cold gray water and almost drowns in his efforts to rescue them? Many men have set down their opinions on this subject, but perhaps the man who has done it best is Arnold Haultain, a Canadian writer who flourished around the turn of the century. Haultain tackled a wide range of subjects from love to Cardinal Newman, but the only book of his that lives on is "The Mystery of Golf". It was first published, in a limited edition, in 1908. Haultain's book—it is really one long, sinuous treatise—apparently did better than was expected, for in 1910

Macmillan brought out a second and somewhat expanded edition. Today, roughly three-quarters of a century later, Haultain's explorations and deductions have lost little of their freshness. It may well be, as some of its admirers have claimed, the equivalent among books on golf to what Izaak Walton's "The Compleat Angler" is to books on fishing.

In the book's second paragraph, Haultain addresses himself to the game's primary mystery; why is it that golf is so endlessly fascinating? He sets the stage for this quite memorably:

> I have just come home from my club. We played until we couldn't see the flag; the caddies were sent ahead to find the balls by the thud of their fall; and a large low moon threw whispering shadows on the dew-wet grass or ere we trode the home-green. At dinner the talk was—of golf. Yet the talkers were neither idiots, fools, or monomaniacs. On the contrary, many of

them were grave men of the world. At all events the most mono-maniacal of the lot was a prosper-ous man of affairs, worth I do not know how many thousands, which thousands he had made by the same mental faculties by which this eve-ning he was trying to probe or to elucidate the profundities and com-plexities of this so-called "game". Will some one tell us wherein lies its mystery?

The author, it is obvious, is an in-tellectual as well as a golfer. (The twain do meet.) This occasionally makes Haultain hard to read. It is unavoidable. Haultain is attempting to use the varied and voluminous knowl-edge he has gleaned through years of study as a means of clarifying the many small mysteries that are part of the overall mystery of golf. En route he resorts to his grasp of anatomy, biolo-gy, physiology, psychology, philoso-phy, and neurology in order to probe as deeply as he can into the heart of the matter and to articulate as clearly as *possible the nature and the meaning of his findings. During certain stretches he demands full concentration, but it is worth the effort. What a fine mind this Edwardian had! How much he knows about many fields of knowledge and many disciplines we think of as relatively modern! These are the very reasons why it probably is advisable to read his report on his quest in comparatively short takes.*

Rather early in his journey, Haultain comes to grips with his subject: he states that he believes that there is no other game that makes as many demands as golf does on the man or woman whose aim is to play it consistently well. As he sees it, a golfer of the first class must not only possess exceptional physical coordination but a probing, attentive mind that works in happy coalescence with the movements of his body, the play of his emotions, and the steadfastness of his purpose. This is a tall order indeed, but Haultain is unquestionably right. All one has to do is to pause and consider the other sports and recreations he plays or has played. If a devotee of tennis, squash, or other racquet games has an off-day, does the level of his play drop as drastically as it does if he loses the groove of his golf swing? Hardly. If a golfer is an all-around athlete who performs rather well at baseball, basketball, football, and the other traditional team sports, does his performance in them on an off-day fall so sharply that he becomes a liability to his team? Very seldom. If he hunts or swims or sails or fences or throws the discus, when he is experiencing an off-day does he look as if he had never previously attempted that diversion? Rarely, if ever. However, every serious golfer has suffered through days when he does everything so badly that it looks as if he has never played the game before. He hooks or slices his tee shots impartially. His approach shots are so wayward that when he hits a crisp iron onto the green, he is unable to explain to himself what he did differently. When he is in a bunker, after failing to get the ball out on three or four attempts, he simply picks it up and heroically does not throw his wedge at the nearest tree. His chip shots stop halfway to the cup or slide off the far edge of the green. He is flawless on the one-foot tap-ins that are conceded, but he cannot hit the cup on a three-foot putt. Haultain knows all this. He has been through it himself. When he analyses the difficulty of golf, he does so as a fellow-sufferer who is out to help his brother.

Haultain is not only a sympathetic observer but a serious entertainer. The most talented writers were the great entertainers in an age that had no motion pictures, no radio, and no television. Some days you could hardly wait for the postman to arrive with the weekly magazine. Haultain knows how to change pace and arrest your attention.

. . . What is there in the game of golf which so differentiates it from all others that in it these trifling minutiae become magnified to matters of great moment? I take it because in golf the mind *plays a highly curious and important part. In cricket, tennis, racquets, polo, the entire absence of such maxims as "Keep your eye on the ball," "Be up," "Slow back," "Follow through," "Don't go to sleep," and the rest of them—all addressed to the mind—shows that in these the mind requires no external or adventitious stimulus. Who would dream of taking his eye off an approaching ball in cricket?—who could do it? Who could possibly go to sleep in the midst of a rally in tennis? Evidently in these games the movement of the ball is sufficient stimulus in itself—it is* the *stimulus. Now, in golf there is no such stimulus, and the mind has to be goaded into action by laborious and incessant iteration of mental formulae dinned into the memory and repeated over and over again. (I know a man who repeats to himself six rules every time he takes*

his driver in hand and addresses the ball.)

Somewhat farther along, Haultain pauses for a moment and then plunges forward and into the heart of his disquisition:

The difficulties of golf are immense. For think for a moment: there is scarcely a muscle in the body that is not called into play; and every muscle is controlled by a nerve. In fact, every muscle is a bundle of fibres or spindles, and every fibre or spindle is controlled by the branch of a nerve, cannot contract save in response to a stimulus conveyed to it by a branch of a nerve. Unless an order is sent from the brain and distributed to each and every part of the machinery which moves the trunk and limbs, not a movement can be made. And to ensure harmonious and coordinate movement, those orders must be very carefully, not only timed, but apportioned.

Thank heavens, after trekking deep into neurology—so deep that you no longer wonder why on some days you look as if you had never played the game before—Haultain steps back a couple of paces and begins to explain that it is the extraordinary demands that golf makes that account for its abiding charm: it discloses the true nature of the man or woman who plays the game; it is such a wonderful game that it is inevitable that golf is now catching on with people of all classes; in the end, forgetting about psychological matters for the moment, it favors the player who combines strength with dexterity; and, in this hard world with its ups and downs, what a priceless possession is golf with the endless beauty of its courses, the genial companionship of the clubhouse, and the game's inexhaustible lure!

After finishing my most recent reading of "The Mystery of Golf", three thoughts of different textures entered

*my mind. The first one was personal:
When I am playing poorly, I usually
have a fairly good idea of the incorrect
movements that are causing my bad
play, but at those rare times when I am
hitting my shots much better than is
normal for me, I have no idea at all
what I am doing that is bringing this
about. Second, I thought of a statement
made by a golfing friend who loves to
exhibit his knowledge. I had pegged
him many years before as a fellow with
a first-class second-class mind. Then
he said something that showed me that
I had underrated him. He said. "Did it
ever strike any of you guys that if you
are the longest hitter in your foursome,
you almost always play pretty good
golf?"*

*And, third, I thought of an experi-
ence Henry Cotton told me about. It
could not have been more Haultanian.
A beautiful striker of the ball from tee
to green, Cotton, a three-time winner of
the British Open, was a good putter,*

but his putting was a discernible level below the rest of his game. Late one afternoon when he was running through some experiments on the practice green at his club, he found himself holing putt after putt, and, what is more, he felt confident that he could go on and on doing this. The club had never before felt quite like this in his hands, and the balls rotated perfectly as they rolled to the hole. He called over to a young man who worked in the pro shop and told him to fetch some brown paper, some thumb tacks, and a pencil. When the young man arrived with Cotton's order, Cotton and he secured the brown paper to the grip of his putter. Cotton then carefully placed his hands on it in the same position he had been using so successfully. For good measure, he walked to the nearest ball and stroked it into the middle of the cup fifteen feet away. Then he asked the young man to trace on the brown paper the exact position of his hands on the shaft. The next morning the first thing Cotton did when he arrived at the club was to pick up the putter and a few balls and go out to the practice green. With the utmost fastidiousness, he placed his hands on the shaft so that his wrists, his thumbs, and his fingers were in the precise position the lines on the brown paper indicated. He stepped up to a ball and putted it. It felt firm, and it rolled nicely over the edge of the cup he was aiming at. He reset his hands and hit another good putt that almost dropped. He rubbed his forehead and sighed. His stoke did not feel at all like the stroke he had stumbled on the day before. He stayed on the practice green another ten minutes, gripping the putter with great deliberation so that everything corresponded to the pencilled tracings on the brown paper. Then he gathered his balls and walked in. He hadn't been able to reproduce the marvelous feel and stroke he had had the day before.

He hadn't been sure the experiment would work, but it had been well worth the try. Anything that can help your golf is.

Herbert Warren Wind

THE MYSTERY OF
GOLF:

A brief account of games in general: their origin, antiquity, and popularity: and of the game called golf in particular: its uniqueness, its curiousness, and its difficulty; its anatomical, philosophical, and moral properties; together with diverse opinions on other matters pertaining to it.

BY ARNOLD HAULTAIN

Boston and New York
HOUGHTON MIFFLIN COMPANY
1 9 0 8

FOUR HUNDRED AND FORTY COPIES

PRINTED AT THE RIVERSIDE PRESS IN 1908

THIS COPY IS NUMBER.....*441*........

CONTENTS

CONTENTS

Contents

THE MYSTERY OF GOLF

" . . . ces jeux où se mêlent merveilleusement,
pour interroger notre fortune, le hasard et la
science; jeux presque mystiques et toujours pas-
sionnants, où l'homme se plaît à tâter sa chance
aux confins de son être."

MAURICE MAETERLINCK.

THE MYSTERY
OF GOLF

HREE things there are as un-
fathomable as they are fascinating to the masculine mind: metaphysics; golf; and the feminine
heart. The Germans, I believe, pretend to
have solved some of the riddles of the first,
and the French to have unravelled some of
the intricacies of the last; will some one tell us
wherein lies the extraordinary fascination of
golf?

I have just come home from my Club. We
played till we could not see the flag; the caddies were sent ahead to find the balls by the
thud of their fall; and a low large moon threw

whispering shadows on the dew-wet grass or ere we trode the home-green. At dinner the talk was of golf; and for three mortal hours after dinner the talk was — of golf. Yet the talkers were neither idiots, fools, nor monomaniacs. On the contrary, many of them were grave men of the world. At all events the most monomaniacal of the lot was a prosperous man of affairs, worth I do not know how many thousands, which thousands he had made by the same mental faculties by which this evening he was trying to probe or to elucidate the profundities and complexities of this so-called ''game.'' Will some one tell us wherein lies its mystery?

I

I AM a recent convert to golf. But it is the recent convert who most closely scrutinizes his creed — as certainly it is the recent convert who most zealously avows it. The old hand is more concerned about how he plays

[2]

than about why he plays; the duffer is puzzled at the extraordinary fascination which
his new-found pass-time exercises over him.
He came to scoff; he remains to play; he
inwardly wonders how it was that he was so
long a heretic; and, if he is a proselyte given
to Higher Criticism, he seeks reasons for the
hope that is in him.

Well, I know a man, whether in the flesh
or out of the flesh I cannot tell, I know such
an one who some years ago joined a golf club,
but did not play. The reasons for so extraordinary a proceeding were simple. The members (of course) were jolly good fellows; the
comfort was assured; the links — the landscape, he called it — were beautiful. But he
did not play. What fun was to be derived from
knocking an insignificant-looking little white
ball about the open country he did not see.
Much less did he see why several hundred
pounds a year should be expended in rolling
and cutting and watering certain patches of

this country, while in others artfully-contrived obstacles should be equally expensively constructed and maintained. Least of all could he understand (he was young then, and given to more violent games) how grown-up men could go to the trouble of travelling far, and of putting on flannels, hob-nailed boots, and red coats, for the simple and apparently effortless purpose of hitting a ball as seldom as possible with no one in the world to oppose his strength or his skill to their hitting; and it seemed to him not a little childish to erect an elaborate club-house, with dressing-rooms, dining-rooms, smoking-rooms, shower-baths, lockers, verandas, and what not, for so simple a recreation, and one requiring so little exertion. Surely marbles would be infinitely more diverting than that. If it were football, now, or even tennis — and he once had the temerity to venture to suggest that a small portion of the links might be set apart for a court — the turf about the home-hole was very tempt-

ing. The dead silence with which this innocent proposition was received gave him pause.
(He sees now that an onlooker might as well
have requested from a whist party the loan of
a few cards out of the pack to play card-tricks
withal.)

Yet it is neither incomprehensible nor irra-
tional, this misconception on the part of the
layman of the royal and antient game of golf.
To the uninitiated, what is there in golf to
be seen? A ball driven of a club; that is all.
There is no exhibition of skill opposed to skill
or of strength contending with strength; there
is apparently no prowess, no strategy, no tac-
tics — no pitting of muscle and brain against
muscle and brain. At least, so it seems to the
layman. When the layman has caught the in-
fection, he thinks — and knows — better.

But, as a matter of fact, contempt could
be poured upon any game by anyone unac-
quainted with that game. We know with what
apathetic contempt Subadar Chinniah or Je-

madar Mohamed Khan looks on while Tommy Atkins swelters as he bowls or bats or fields under a broiling Indian sun, or Tommy's subalterns kick up the maidan's dust with their polo-ponies' hoofs. And what could be more senseless to a being wholly ignorant of cards than the sight of four grey-headed men gravely seating themselves before dinner to arrange in certain artificial combinations certain uncouth pictures of kings and queens and knaves and certain spots of red and black? Not until such a being recognizes the infinite combinations of chance and skill possible in that queen of sedentary games does he comprehend the fascination of whist. And so it is with golf. All that is requisite in golf, so it seems to the onlooker, is to hit; and than a "hit" nothing, surely, can be simpler or easier — so simple and easy that to have a dozen sticks to hit with, and to hire a boy to carry them, is not so much a sign of pitiable insanity as of wilful stupidity. The puerility of the proceeding is enough to make the spectator irate. Especially as, owing to the silence and the seriousness with which the golfer plays, and his reticence as to the secret of the game — for none knows better than the golfer that the game renders up its secret only to the golfer, if even to him — this quiet, red-coated individual is surrounded with a sort of halo of superiority, a halo not made by himself. No wonder the onlooker's anger is aroused. That expertness in puerility of this sort should of itself exalt a man, make him possessed of that which obviously, yet unintentionally, raises him above the intelligent yet indignant onlooker — there is something in this past finding out. Nor does he find it out till he himself is converted. Golf is like faith: it is the substance of things hoped for, the evidence of things not seen; and not until it is personally experienced does the unbelieving change from the imprecatory to the precatory attitude.

However, the erstwhile aforesaid non-play-

ing member of the golf club in question, the
suppleness of his epiphyses, it may be, be-
coming (perhaps not quite imperceptibly) un-
equal to the activity and agility demanded of
them by more ardent games, purchased, first
one club, then another, then a sheaf, and be-
took himself to the task of finding out *a poste-*
riori, by the experimental method, what there
was in the confounded game that brought the
players there by scores to play. — And to talk
of their play. For it should be added that the
talk at that club puzzled him as much as the
play. It was not enough that keen King's
Counsel, grave judges, erudite men of letters,
statesmen, and shrewd men of business should
play as if the end of life were to hole a ball; but
they talked as if the way a ball should be holed
were the only knowledge worth possessing.
Well, he played; or, to be more precise, he
attempted to play, and, fortunately for him,
he persevered in the attempt. Then indeed did
the scales fall from his eyes. He discovered

[8]

that there was more in golf than met the eye
— much more.

II

How great a similarity there is in all outdoor
human games! Probably ninety per cent. of
human outdoor games consist in the propul-
sion of a spherical or spheroidal object towards
a certain spot. In cricket, rounders, football,
baseball, polo, basket-ball, croquet, marbles,
tennis, racquets, quoits, billiards, bagatelle,
fives, pool, curling, lacrosse, hockey, ping-
pong, golf, either one party assails with a ball,
a sphere, a spheroid, or a disc a position de-
fended by another, or both parties assail with
a similar object the selfsame position, victory
lying with the party reaching it first. It would
be interesting to dive into the primæval origin
of games and to discuss whether the first distinct differentiation of the man from the ape
consisted not in the ability to throw a stone
and wield a bough, to attack with a sphere and

[9]

defend with a stick, the pithecanthropoid prototypes of batting and bowling. The first ape that tried to possess himself of a fruit he could not reach, or to repel a foe he could not grapple, by throwing a stone or using a branch, was in all probability the progenitor of the human race. It may, indeed, be that man's erect posture was gradually evolved by this attempt to throw and wield (which could not be done on all fours), and that the ape became the true ἄνθρωπος—the true "face-up-turning" animal (ἀνὰ — πρέπω — ὤψ) — when he succeeded in hurling and hitting. In the case of this supposititious ape, the throwing and hitting were actions primarily prompted by hunger or love, by the desire to obtain food or by the desire to obtain a mate (or to keep off a rival)—the two primal instincts of life. In so far they were highly utilitarian.

With all due deference to Schiller and to Herbert Spencer, with their theory of the "play instinct" as at the bottom of all art, I contend that all our amusements, like all our art, derive ultimately from the most serious, most utilitarian instincts. In the world of life, mere play, *quâ* play, is as non-existent as, in the world of nature, is mere beauty, *quâ* beauty. Beauty is but the perfection of useful matter. The most lovely landscape is but hills and dales and trees. The most wonderful human body is but bone and muscle and fascia and nerve. There is nothing in nature, and there is nothing in the anatomical frame, put there for beauty's sake alone. All is for use; nothing for ornament. And as art is but the reproduction, the representation, of the perfection of useful nature, so sport is but a reproduction, the representation of the perfection of useful occupation. Even the gambols of kittens and puppies are the hereditary and instinctive reproduction of contests with teeth or claws. In this sense only, in piping times of peace, when man was not afraid of his fellow-man, can man be said to have "played" with his fellow-man — contended with him in amicable and imitative combat. — They are near akin, are art and sport; the one being the intellectual and emotional, the other the muscular and nervous, representation of the primal and highly utilitarian instincts of hunger and love exerting themselves, in the form of hunting and mating and fighting, in a world of animal and vegetable life.

All masculine games are contests. Whether there are any such things as feminine games proper is doubtful. When girls play games they play with their brothers, or they play their brothers' games. And even when they play among themselves, their games prove the evolutionary law, and show themselves to be refinements on primæval feminine occupations: they play at "doll's-house," at "school," at "mistress and maid"; they pay visits to one another, they dress up in their elders' clothes, they make mud-pies, they erect diminutive domiciles, they nurse unheeding dolls. Of these the derivation is obvious.

One other species of games there is, but as into it little or no element of sport enters, it needs not to be classified here. To gamble is perhaps as primæval an instinct as to fight. Herr Karl Groos, indeed, regards gambling as a sort of fight against fate. In almost all games, too, an element of chance inheres — inheres, and thus perhaps enhances the interest of the game. But it is a question whether a game of mere and sheer chance deserves the name. Rouge et Noir is hardly a "game"; a sport it certainly is not.

You can detect national character in games. Golf is preëminently the game of the Scot: slow, sure, quiet, deliberate, canny even — each man playing for himself. There is no defensive play, no attacking an enemy's position, no subordination of oneself to the team, no captain to be obeyed, no relative positions of players. Compare with it cricket, the game

typical of the Anglo-Saxon of more southern
proclivities. Here you have more excitement,
greater rapidity of action. There is no serious
and contemplative addressing of yourself to
the ball; no terrible anxiety over your stance;
no forty-two rules for your slog. Golf, on the
other hand, is self-reliant, silent, sturdy. It
leans less on its fellows. It loves best to overcome obstacles alone. If the golfer take a caddie, it but proves him a member of a clan:
his caddie is his fellow-clansman. Of the two,
perhaps cricket is for youth the superior game.
It requires as keen an eye, as accurate an adjustment of hand and eye, as great muscular
power in the stroke, and it is more rapid. It
must be played, too, as much as golf, "with
the heid." In cricket you have an ally or
allies, both in batting and fielding; it is com-
munistic, political. The nation that evolved
cricket evolved the British constitution.

Note, too, an you will, the nomenclature
proper to golf. Where your blunt and careless

Southron cricketer "slogs" or "blocks" or is "stumped," your Northern golfing precisian religiously takes his "stance," "addresses" himself to the ball, and "approaches" the hole; — a phraseology smacking of the Assembly of Divines. There is something Puritanically and Sinaitically threatening in the thought of "approaching" a hole; as if, puir aperture, it were not to be come at but after due preparation thereunto, and were altogether fenced off from the ignorant, the scandalous, and the profane. And so indeed it is: the hole is an ominous and portentous ordinance, and often mightily inconveniently placed; and the duffer who thinks to enter therein without much searching of heart, without diligent use of all means suitable and answerable unto so high and serious a task, if he doth not thereby render himself liable to admonishment by his elders, is nevertheless, in the matter of the "approach," still in the eenfancy of golf!

III

THERE is rampant in the world at the present moment a sort of sporting mania, an international sporting mania; excellent in its way, but very difficult to analyse or account for. Manias of one kind or another are not unknown to history. Such, for example, was the mania for Crusades in the Middle Ages. It had a highly rational basis, namely the defence of Christendom against Islam and the wresting of the Holy Land from its desecrating possessors. But to such lengths did this mania go that in 1212 an army of children once actually set out, with banners and paraphernalia, to conquer some vague, invisible foe; with the result that hundreds died before they had gone any distance, and hundreds were sold into slavery. Such, too, was the Hippodrome mania in the fourth century at Byzantium, when feeling ran so high that society was divided into hostile sections, and money, and even blood, was recklessly spent in contests between the faction of the Green and the faction of the Blue. And such was the tulip mania of Holland in 1637, when, so keen was the rivalry for bulbs, that a whole nation was absorbed in the strife and many a family ruined itself by speculation in rare or mythical roots.

Well, to-day the western world seems to be labouring under something of the same sort. Year by year athletics occupy a larger share of the attention, not only of the students, but of the teachers, at our schools and colleges, and year by year the sums spent in intercollegiate and international contests increase. To win a comparatively valueless cup by means of a comparatively unserviceable craft, a single individual spends some millions of sesterces, and two nations look on intent on the race and applaud. Teams without number, of all kinds, cross and re-cross the Atlantic and Pacific; money is poured out like water on race-horses,

[17]

motor-cars, dirigible balloons, and what-not.
—Like the Crusades, there is for all this a
highly rational basis, that most laudable one
of amicable rivalry in brain or muscle; but,
like the Crusades, it is a question whether it
is not here and there just a little overdone.

IV

And yet, why is it, let us ask ourselves, that
mankind consents to hold prowess in sport
in such high esteem? From the days of the
Olympian and Isthmian games to the latest
broken record, always athletic excellence has
elicited spontaneous admiration. To the champion, to him who excels in any kind of game,
—the batsman, the oarsman, the boxer,—we
look up with a certain sort of awe, an instinctive and mysterious sort of worship. The feeling is deep-seated and universal; it must have
its roots far down in the primitive foundations
of human history and human nature.

Well, if my theory that all sport is but amicable combat is correct, prowess in games is proof and symbol of prowess in that inevitable and sempiternal combat of man with man and of man with nature without which neither would mankind as a whole have evolved, nor would special races of men have emerged and dominated the world. Men seem instinctively to understand that to excel in strength or agility means much more than possession of mere strength or agility; that it means staying-power, will, determination, courage — a host of, not only muscular, but mental and even moral qualities. It was with quite serious, though perhaps shapeless, motives, that the Greeks erected statues to their Olympian victors; motives identical probably with those that led to the deification of Herakles and Thor and all the strong men of mythology.

What may be the particular weapon wielded by the champion matters little, whether bat or ball, boxing-glove, driver, or oar. The weapon is but the medium of his strength and skill, the vehicle of his thought and knowledge. The weapon is to the sportsman what the brush is to the artist or the pen to the poet. It is that by which he shows to the world what manner of man he is. What manner of man he is! That, surely, after all, is the question of questions. It is at the bottom of all religions, which fight among themselves in their theories as to what man's true nature is and how it shall be improved; it is at the bottom of all philosophies, which make desperate and futile efforts to define man and to specify his place in the cosmos; in a way it is at the bottom of all art, since art tries to depict man, or if it depicts Nature, depicts man's conception of her; and it is at the very bottom of sport, than which only the mortal and immemorial conflict of man with man and of mankind with Nature, of which sport is but the symbol and analogue, is a better exponent of the true and secret character of man his real and inner self.

[20]

THE CLUE TO THE MYSTERY

V

THIS modern rampancy of sport does not explain the fascination of golf. No; but it may help to explain its existence. Golf is some hundreds of years old; but only in the last two or three decades has it obtained its extraordinary footing. The interesting question is, Why is it that, amongst the thousand-and-one games to-day played by men, women, and children in Europe and America, why is it that golf commands so large a share of attention, of serious and thoughtful attention? The literature of golf is now immense, and, much of it, good. Eminent men have devoted to it serious study; mathematicians try to solve its problems; prime ministers play it; multimillionaires resort to it; and grown men the world over jeopardize for it name and fame and fortune. Not even bridge quite so absorbs its votaries. Cricketers, foot-ballers, tennis-players do not so utterly abandon homes and offices for the crease, the field, or the lawn. Only the golfer risks everything so he may excel in putting little balls into little holes. — What is the clue to the mystery?

The clue is a compound one. To begin with, it is threefold : physiological; psychological; social. — In the first place, no other game has so simple an object or one requiring, apparently, so simple an exertion of muscular effort. To knock a ball into a hole — that seems the acme of ease. It is a purely physiological matter of moving your muscles *so*, thus the tyro argues ; and in order to move his muscles *so*, he expends more time and money and thought and temper than he cares, at the year's end, to compute. Without doubt the ball must be impelled by muscular movement : how to co-ordinate that muscular movement — that is the physiological factor in the fascination of golf.

In the second place, when the novice begins to give some serious consideration to the game, he discovers that there is such a thing as style in golf, and that a good style results in good golf. He begins to think there must be some recondite knack in the game, a knack that has to be learned by the head and taught by the head to the muscles. Accordingly he takes lessons, learns rules, reads books, laboriously thinks out every stroke, and by degrees comes to the conclusion that mind or brain has as much to do with the game as have hand and eye. — It is here that the psychological factor comes in.

In the third place, having progressed a bit, having learned with a certain degree of skill to manipulate his several clubs; having learned also, and being able with more or less precision to put into practice, certain carefully conned rules as to how he shall stand and how he shall swing, the beginner — for he is still a beginner — discovers that he has not yet learned everything. He discovers that the character of his opponent and the quality of his opponent's play exercise a most extraordinary influence over him. Does he go out with a greater duffer than himself, unconsciously he finds himself growing over-confident or careless. Does he go out with a redoubtable player, one whose name on the Club Handicap stands at Scratch, he cannot allay a certain exaltation or trepidation highly noxious to his game. And it is in vain that he attempts to reason these away. Not only so, but even after months of practice, when the exaltation or trepidation is under control, often it will happen that an opponent's idiosyncrasies will so thoroughly upset him that he will vow never to play with that idiosyncratic again. This we may call the social or moral element. It affects the feelings or the emotions; it affects the mind through these feelings or emotions; and, through the mind, it affects the muscles.

Now, I take it that there is no other game in which these three fundamental factors—

the physiological, the psychological, and the social or moral—are so extraordinarily combined or so constantly called into play. Some sports, such as football, polo, rowing, call chiefly for muscular activity, judgment, and nerve; others, such as chess, draughts, backgammon, call upon the intellect only. In no other game that I know of is, first, the whole anatomical frame brought into such strenuous yet delicate action at every stroke; or, second, does the mind play so important a part in governing the actions of the muscles; or, third, do the character and temperament of your opponent so powerfully affect you as they do in golf. To play well, these three factors in the game must be most accurately adjusted, and their accurate adjustment is as difficult as it is fascinating.

VI

ALL true games, I have said, are contests. But in golf the contest is not with your fellow-man. The foe in golf is not your opponent, but great Nature herself, and the game is to see who will over-reach her better, you or your opponent. In almost all other games you pit yourself against a mortal foe; in golf it is yourself against the world: no human being stays your progress as you drive your ball over the face of the globe. It is very like life in this, is golf. Life is not an internecine strife. We are all here fighting, not against each other for our lives, but against Nature for our livelihoods. In golf we can see a symbol of the history and fate of human kind: careering over the face of this open earth, governed by rigid rule, surrounded with hazards, bound to subdue Nature or ere we can survive, punished for the minutest divergence from the narrow course, and the end of it all. . . . And the end of it all? . . . To reach an exiguous grave with as few mistakes as may be — some with high and brilliant flight, others with slow and lowly crawl. . . .

VII

To descend, however, from this highly abstract plane, why is it, let us ask, that golf to so many of us seems to-day a game unique?

Well, amongst other things, it is unique because it is so difficult. Curiously enough, its chief difficulty arises from its chief simplicity. In golf you hit a stationary ball. At first blush that sounds the acme of ease. It is not; though it takes even a zealot some days to plumb the depths of that paradox. At first blush it would seem that a cricket ball—flying towards you, its trajectory foreshortened, its velocity variable, its pitch problematical, its break uncertain—would be of all balls the hardest to hit; and the next hardest, seemingly, would be the racquet or the tennis ball. All three come fast, and you never know exactly whence they are coming or whither they are going. The difficulties in cricket, racquets, and tennis seem immense. Yet they are not as great as the dif-

[27]

ficulties in golf. If they were, we should surely
ere this have been, in this analytical era, in-
undated with theoretic lucubrations as to how
these should be played, as assuredly we have
been in the matter of golf. Besides, no cricketer suffers agonies in debating with himself
of the correctness of his stance, or of the character of his swing; or addresses himself with
painful pause to the bowling; or waggles his
implement with serious, not to say solemn, in-
sistence; or devoutly locks up a pet bat against
the day of some extra-important match; or
requires from all spectators of his play the
most awesome and reverential silence. What
is there in the game of golf which so differentiates it from all others that in it these trifling
minutiæ become magnified to matters of great
moment? I take it it is because in golf the
mind plays a highly curious and important
part. In cricket, tennis, racquets, polo, the entire absence of such maxims as "Keep your
eye on the ball," "Be up," "Slow back,"

"Follow through," "Don't go to sleep,"
and the rest of them—all addressed to the
mind—shows that in these the mind requires
no external or adventitious stimulus. Who
would dream of taking his eye off an approaching ball in cricket?—who could do it?
Who could possibly go to sleep in the midst
of a rally in tennis? Evidently in these games
the movement of the ball is sufficient stimulus
in itself—it is *the* stimulus. Now, in golf
there is no such stimulus, and the mind has
to be goaded into attention and action by laborious and incessant iteration of mental formulæ dinned into the memory and repeated
over and over again. (I know a man who repeats to himself six rules every time he takes
his driver in hand and addresses the ball.)
This is curious, but it is true; and perhaps
the following train of reasoning will substan-
tiate the assertion. No game can be played
without accurate and delicate adjustment of
hand and eye; this adjustment is primarily

[29]

the function, through the nerves, of the mind;
it cannot be achieved unless the mind is in-
stantly and constantly stimulated to action;
in all rapid games the movement of the ball
supplies this stimulus, for it excites the perceptive faculties, and, through them, the conceptive, by which the orders for the next stroke
are issued; in golf there is little or no excita-
tion of the perceptive faculties; accordingly
the conceptive faculties have to be concentrated and roused to action by artful and
adventitious means, by precepts learned by
rote and forcibly applied at every stroke. That
is the psychology of golf. In all quick games,
so strong and so rapid are the stimuli that the
resulting movements might almost be called
reflex or automatic. Volleying at the net in
tennis might certainly be so called: there is no
time to think; the very sight of the approaching ball throws the right arm into position to
receive and strike it. To the expert tennis-
player the movement is doubtless reflex and

automatic, as automatic as the closing of the eyelid on the approach of a fly—though both, probably, are the result of constant response to stimulus. Now, in golf there is never any reflex action possible. Every stroke must be played by the mind—gravely, quietly, deliberately. And this is why there is a psychology of golf but there is no psychology of cricket or racquets or tennis or polo. If for this theory it is necessary to show that strong stimulation of the perceptive faculties tends to strong stimulation of the conceptive, one might point to the effect of music upon the mind and body. How easy it is to dance when the rhythmic valse strikes upon the ear! what waves of thought and emotion are set agoing at sound of martial airs!

VIII

As a matter of fact most of the difficulties in golf are mental, not physical; are subjective, not objective; are the created phantasms of the mind, not the veritable realities of the course. Bad lies, on good links, are the exception, not the rule; and bunkers are avowedly where they are in order to catch the unworthy and the unwary. That wood to the right is no real obstacle to your drive; why then are you so fearful of a slice? Were you blindfold and could not see it, it would be as if it were not, and the so-called "difficulty" would vanish. And yet the number of balls that do go into that wood — or are pulled off to the left to avoid it — is astonishing. — The mere test of strength or of skill is one of the most subordinate of the elements of golf; much more important is the test of what goes by the name of "nerve," that quiet self-confidence which no ghostly phantasms can shake, in howsoever questionable shape they come. So many golfers forget this. "If I had not done this, that, or the other stupid thing," they say, "my score would have been so-and-so." My dear sir, it is just those stupid things that make the game. Eliminate the liability of the frail and peccant human mind to do stupid things, and you might as well play pitch and toss. It is this very frailty and peccability of the human mind that golf calls in question, and it is this that differentiates golf from all other games, because in golf this frailty is shown in its utter nudity, not hidden away under cover of agility or excitement or concerted action, as it is in cricket or football or tennis or polo or what-not. The simplicity of the thing to be done strips the soul of all cloak of excuse for not doing it. You may place your ball how or where you like, you may hit it with any sort of implement you like; all you have to do is to hit it into a hole. Could simpler conditions be devised? Could an easier task be essayed? And yet, such is the extraordinary constitution of the human golfing soul, that it not only fails to achieve it, but invents for itself multiform and manifold ifs and ans for

[33]

not achieving it: ifs and ans the nature and number of which must assuredly move the laughter of the gods. . . . I have often thought that golf was the invention of the de—well, let us say, of the deities of Olympus, an invention contrived for a twofold purpose: first to afford them subject-matter for merriment; and second to prove to vaunting man how trivial a creature he is. —In my mind's eye I can see brawny Zeus, with stout Hera at his side (she must be inclining to *embonpoint* by this time), lying beside his nectar and watching puny men chasing pigmy balls over this paltry planet. What inextinguishable laughter must ring through the Sacred Mount at sight of grave statesmen and puissant potentates, mighty satraps and great pro-consuls, Right Reverends and Right Honourables, striving strenuously to put little pieces of india-rubber into little holes in the ground, and "damnin' awfu'" when they don't! . . .

IX

However, probably neither the youthful caddie nor the elderly professional is much given to any very minute analysis of the mental factors incident to golf. It is only he who takes up golf when well past his 'teens who finds that the motor centres have carefully to be taught and trained by the ideational centres; and probably not until the motor centres have learned to act largely by themselves does such golfer improve in his game. Probably, the more automatically one plays, the better one plays—which means that (unless one is a born athlete, or a muscular genius) one ought to commence golf very young indeed. (Zealous golfers had better enter their babies' names on the waiting lists of limited clubs.) For I take it that if the mind is strenuously occupied in trying to remember this, that, or the other particular rule for the stroke, some other rules are apt to be forgotten. That is to

[35]

say, if the ideational or conceptual centres of the brain are too much occupied, some motor centres go disregarded. In the caddie and the professional probably at the moment of the stroke there is no ideation or conception going on whatsoever, the whole attention of the mind being in some incomprehensible way concentrated on the motor centres alone. All beginners — of a maturer age — find it impossible to remember — and obey — at every stroke all the rules they learn. — "What on earth," said one fair golfer to another once, "do you wear that ring on your thumb for?" — "To remind me of a certain rule." — "Good gracious!" said the other, "*I* should have to wear rings on my fingers and bells on my toes to remind me of all the rules I forget!"

I asked an admirable professional once, a man whose skill in tuition equalled his skill with the clubs, who thought out each stroke and excelled in the ætiology and diagnosis of the faults of his pupils, — I asked this professional to try to tell me precisely what it was that passed through his mind in that important but minute interval of time which elapsed between the raising of his club for the backswing and its impact with the ball. He promised to do his best to find out, and his answer was as significant as it was practical. "I canna find oot, Sorr," he said some days afterwards; "I dinna think I think aboot anything at a'. I juist luke at me ba'. Ef I do not luke at me ba', the stroke disna coom aff." Of an amateur to whom I put the same quæry, the reply was to the effect that if his mental attitude was at all reducible to verbal phraseology, it would probably take the form of the prayer of that Publican, who did not lift up so much as his eyes unto heaven, but smote upon his breast, saying, "God be merciful to me a sinner."

In one respect the professional and the caddie have an immense advantage over the amateur in golf: they are handling golf-clubs all day long; if they are not swinging them, they are making or mending them; they do nothing that tends to develope any set of muscles other than those brought into play in the game. And this is no unimportant point. The amateur rides or rows or shoots or yachts or fishes. Now, it may be a preposterous thing to assert, a thing that may arouse the derision of all but enthusiasts of the game, but it is highly probable that any form of exercise which brings into play and developes muscles not used in golf, or not used in the way that golf uses them, is injurious, not beneficial, to the golfer. If neither a violinist nor a pianist would dream of developing the muscles of his forearm and wrist by, say, hoeing or digging, neither should a golfer. I once knew a man who for a whole snowy winter did not touch a club, but daily visited a gymnasium and went through a variety of exercises for the express purpose of developing his muscles for his summer's golf—his ambition was long driving.

What was the consequence? He confessed to me that that summer he was completely off his game! Another man I knew whose sole form of exercise that winter was walking and swinging golf clubs. This man's game improved vastly. The explanation probably lies in the fact that the nerve-currents by which the muscles are contracted are very prone to run in the tracks to which they are habituated; and if for several weeks or months they are made to travel in paths quite different from those in which they must run—and swiftly and accurately run—in the drive and the approach and the put, when they are ordered to take the new direction they fail at first to find it. No stoker or coal-heaver could suddenly become a card engraver; and if a card engraver took to stoking or coal-heaving, he would probably turn out very unsaleable visiting-cards when first he returned to his vocation. Everybody has noticed how persistently the cricketing stroke sticks to the cricketer who drops cricket for golf in maturer years. — This anatomical frame of ours is a wonderful machine; we little know what slaves we are to it. — The curious thing about golf is that adepts in all sorts of other and alien forms of sport think that there is no reason under heaven why they should not compel their anatomical frames to comply with the demands made upon them by the links. They excel, so they argue, in cricket or tennis or racquets, why not in this ridiculously easy task of putting a ball into a hole? And when they fail, they become exasperated — and spend pounds in lessons — and pounds in implements of curious make — goose-necked putters, Schenectady putters, socket-headed drivers, aluminium cleeks — of these the name is Legion! There is not a game known to sportsmen in which failure so exasperates. Nay, it is not a game, if by "game" we mean a mere pass-time. Or, if it is, it is a method of passing the time than which few serious vocations so absorb the faculties, mental, moral, and physical; or (shall we say?) so develope them. At least it is a game in which earnestness, that moral attribute of character which seems now-a-days sometimes in serious danger of disparagement, in which earnestness ranks so high that, we may safely say, without it success is impossible. —I once heard of a lady champion who, in solitude, wept in sheer nervous tension over her victory. All honour to her tears!

X

However, after all this abstruse metaphysical and anatomical disquisition, shall we essay to discover practically what it is at bottom makes a man play well and what it is makes a man play ill; and what it is makes a man one day play well, and the next day ill? —Ah! he who could answer such quæries would tear the veil from Maia. Some men there be, of course, who will never play golf. Either they have a

poor "eye"; or their muscular sense is but
imperfectly developed; or their keenness in
sport is nil; or they are too much taken up
with the things of this world; or they are men
wrapt up in the contemplation of so-called
higher things. University professors I have
known who, when they ought to have had
their eye upon the ball, had their eye upon the
clouds, and their minds farther off still. Other
men I have known to whom a round of golf
was so casual and frivolous a pass-time that
they would seek to relieve the tædium of the
game (and perhaps entertain you!) by the
narration between strokes of interminable
and pointless anecdotes. Never by such men
will the Royal and Antient Game be properly
played. By such men golf may be given up at
once and for ever. For maugre all appearances
to the contrary, golf is one of the most serious
of sports. As well try to study metaphysics
indifferently, or to attack the feminine heart
indiscreetly, as try to play golf listlessly. One

cannot serve golf and Mammon. Golf is the
most jealous of mistresses. Are you worried
and distrait; are you in debt and expecting
a dun; are stocks unsteady and your margin
small; is a note falling due; or has a more
than ordinarily delicate feminine entangle-
ment gone somewhat awry? Go not near the
links. Take a country walk, or go for a ride;
drop into the Club and ask numerous friends
to assuage their thirst; —do anything rather
than attempt the simple task of putting a little
ball into a little hole. For to put that little ball
into that little hole — or rather into those eighteen little holes — requires — requires what?
Alas! so many things, so many unthought-of
things. It requires, in the first place, a mind
absolutely imperturbed, imperturbable. You
may play chess or bridge or polo or poker on
the eve of bankruptcy; I defy you to play golf
on the eve of a curtain lecture. It takes a
strong character to play strong golf. Golf is as
accurate an ethical criterion of a man as is the

Decalogue. Perhaps this is why your rigid and Puritanical Scots Presbyterian plays so admirably. An eminent Scots philosopher once told me that the eminence of Scottish philosophy (note the Scottish appraisal of things Scottish, an you will) was due to the fact that Scots philosophers were brought up on the Shorter Catechism. I venture to think he might have extended his axiom to the St. Andrews game. — But, not to beat about the bush, this much is certain : golf is a game in which attitude of mind counts for incomparably more than mightiness of muscle. Given an equality of strength and skill, the victory in golf will be to him who is captain of his soul. Give me a clear eye, a healthy liver, a strong will, a collected mind, and a conscience void of offence both toward God and toward men, and I will back the pigmy against the giant. Golf is a test, not so much of the muscle, or even of the brain and nerves of a man, as it is a test of his inmost veriest self; of his soul and spirit; of his whole character and disposition; of his temperament; of his habit of mind; of the entire content of his mental and moral nature as handed down to him by unnumbered multitudes of ancestors. Does his pedigree date back to Romantic heroes — Frankish horsemen or Provençal Knights? Let him see to it that he curbs his impulsive Southern ardour. Does he trace his descent to the Vikings of the North, strenuous sea-kings that roamed afar and devasted foreign shores? Let him see to it that he applies himself to tasks more close at hand, that he wins him nearer victories. Is he a stolid Goth, bull-necked and big of loin? Let him see to it that the more agile-witted Kelt does not wrest victory from him by a deftness more delicate.

XI

BUT all this, again, is vague, theoretic, abstruse. What you, my confidential reader, seek, I know, is some simple, intelligible, practicable rule by which to determine how you, when you telegraph to an opponent and propose a match, shall be able to play transcendently well. What is it, precisely, that will enable you to go round under eighty to-day?—Confidential reader, did ever you hear tell of the elixir of life? Did ever you hear tell of the universal solvent? of the philosopher's stone? of the Sphinx her riddle? or of Fortunatus his cap? Mayhap you have. But mayhap you do not know that the secret of success in golf is more recondite, far more recondite, than is any one of these. These be bagatelles compared with that. A greater fortune awaits him who will discover and divulge the mystery of golf than that which awaits him who will square the circle, explain the potentialities of radium, or solve the problem of the perpetuity of motion.—For, mark you, it is not against the fellow-man his human opponent that the golfer really wars. Nor is it even against Bogey that he pits his skill. The contest is with himself. There is no reason known amongst men why any golfer should ever get into a bunker. He knows, or he thinks he knows, exactly how every stroke in the round should be played. He may carry as many clubs as he likes, clubs of the most flagitious and flamboyant make. Most potent, grave, and reverend signors will stand stock-still and dumb the while he drives; and no thing on this terraqueous globe be permitted to impede his play. A sanguine flag gratuitously points out for him the hole; overtly printed on the sand-box or the score-card is the distance; his blameless ball (over the making of which countless rival manufacturers have expended an ingenuity extreme) lies meekly at his feet — could Nature, or Art, or the Invention of Man farther go to expedite his way? It is Nature, it is Bogey, that are handicapped, not he; — and perchance it is the cognizance of the enormity of the responsibility thus laid upon him that appals the timorous golfer. The conditions are simple in the extreme: to knock a ball into a hole; and damp sand, and mown fields, and rolled greens, and caddie, and professional, and flag —to say nothing of cobbler's-wax, and rosin, and chalk, and hob-nails, and a red coat—contribute to aid him in coping with his foe. — Against whom do you contend if not against yourself?

Ah! But the conditions are the same for your opponent also. There's the rub. He too, therefore, wages a warfare against self. Accordingly golf resolves itself into this: —It is not a wrestle with Bogey; it is not a struggle with your mortal foe; it is a physiological, psychological, and moral fight with yourself; it is a test of mastery over self; and the ultimate and irreducible element of the game is to determine which of the players is the more worthy combatant. You try to prove to your opponent that you are a better man than he;

and your opponent tries to prove to you that he is a better man than you; and the ordeal is decided by competition with a mutual and ideal foe, a foe merciless and implacable, a foe impeccable and impartial, and that will by no means clear the guilty. Golf is the refined modern equivalent of the ancient barbarous Ordeal. To support our claims to superiority to-day, we do not walk blind-fold and bare-foot over nine red-hot plough-shares, we invite our opponent to beat us in putting a ball into eighteen holes; and we look to Pan — in the shape of bunkers and hazards — to Defend the Right; — and Pan is as inexorable as the plough-shares.

XII

GOLF seems to bring the man, the very inmost man, into contact with the man, the very inmost man. In football and hockey you come into intimate — and often forcible enough —

contact with the outer man; chess is a clash
of intellects; but in golf character is laid bare
to character. This is why so many friend-
ships — and some enmities — are formed on
the links. In spite of the ceremony with which
the game is played: the elaborate etiquette,
the punctilious adhesion to the honour, the
enforced silence during the address, the rigid
observance of rules, few if any games so strip
a man of the conventional and the artificial.
In a single round you can sum up a man, can
say whether he be truthful, courageous, hon-
est, upright, generous, sincere, slow to anger
— or the reverse. — Of these arcana of golf
the uninitiated onlooker knows nothing. Yet
if ever that onlooker is initiated into these
Eleusinian mysteries, he changes his mind
and sees in the links a school for the disciplinary exercise of a cynical or stoical self-com-
mand rivalling that of the Cynosarges or the
Porch.

Not only is golf an excellent test of character, it is also an excellent medicament for character. If we only know it, there is a whole Materia Medica between sand-box and flag. The volatile can find, if he will, a sedative; the phlegmatic, an alterative; the neurasthenic, a tonic. And it is a test of character in more ways than one: the cheat simply could not play golf: in the last resort, no one would play with him. It is also a test of tact. Many a man has to learn how to lend a deaf ear politely to a loquacious friend, or to curb his own tongue when playing with a taciturn one; and probably there is no one but has had on some occasion or other to keep his own temper sweet while the atmosphere about him was mephitic with a surly silence or rent by vituperative abuse.

XIII

The two best schools for mind and manners, says the sage, are the Court and the Camp. He might have added a third. He who would attain self-knowledge should frequent the links. If one seriously essays the task, one will "find oneself" in golf. Few things better reveal a man to himself than zealous and persistent efforts to decrease his handicap. That profound and ancient maxim γνῶθι σεαυτόν, a maxim so ancient and profound that Juvenal averred it had descended from heaven (*Sat.* xi, 27), might be inscribed on the portal of every Golf Club. Even it might be said that Tennyson's trinity of excellences, self-knowledge, self-reverence, self-control, are nowhere so worthily sought, or so efficacious when found, as on the links. — To the Greeks this will be foolishness; to golfers a platitudinous truism.

For golf must be played "conscientiously" — so an eminent King's Counsel once remarked to me. He was right. The duffer imagines that at the very most it only requires a good "hand and eye" and some sort of knack. A good eye and a very large amount of skill it certainly does need; but he who thinks that these are the Alpha and Omega of golf will be apt to remain a duffer long. Between this Alpha and this Omega is a whole alphabet. Golf requires the most concentrated mental attention. It requires also just as concentrated a moral attention. The moral factors in the game are as important as the physical. He who succumbs to temptation will have to succumb to defeat. *Satis imperat*, says an old adage, *qui sibi est imperiosus:* he rules enough who rules himself. This should be the motto of every golfer. "If one man conquer in battle a thousand times a thousand men," says the Dhammapada with oriental extravagance, "and if another conquer himself, he is the greatest of conquerors," a text which is brought home to one in every round. "Greater," said Solomon, "is he that ruleth himself than he that taketh a city." In golf the ruler of himself will take many a hole.—And in truth the golfer knows this, and many and curious sometimes are the means he adopts to attain this end. Every reader will recall the idiosyncrasies of his friends, even if he cannot recall his own: how one will regale himself on stout and steak, and another lunch off chicken and tea; how Robinson will order a tankard of ale, and Anderson a tumbler of Scotch; how Bibulus will challenge Asceticus to take another helping of pie, and Asceticus respond by challenging Bibulus to wash it down with liqueur; how Fumosus will smoke cigars or cigarettes the whole round through, and Abstemius resolutely leave his pipe in his locker; how Medicus will seek by diet or drugs to eliminate this or that unheard-of acid from his frame, and Hereticus live high to accomplish the same purpose.—The cellar and the pantry of a Golf Club, an they would, could divulge many a tale. And all, what for? To "bring under," as Saint Paul saith, this pervicacious body of ours, or to brace this puny soul of ours to the conflict so that we shall not "beat the air," as saith Saint Paul again.

XIV

THE thousand and one things that we should *not* do in golf are evidence of the difficulties of the game. In no other game must immense strength go hand in hand with extreme delicacy. If a fraction of a square inch of wood or steel does not come in contact with a fraction of a cubic inch of gutta-percha exactly *so* and not otherwise, you are landed in a bunker, or you fly off to one side, or you overrun the hole. And in every stroke in golf this nicety of accuracy is necessary. If in the Drive the whole weight and strength of the body, from the nape of the neck to the soles of the feet, are not transferred from body to ball through the minute and momentary contact of club with ball absolutely surely, yet swiftly —you top, or you pull, or you sclaff, or you slice, or you swear (let us hope episcopally: which, being interpreted, according to the anecdote, signifieth silently). So with the Put.

Not even an expert dare be careless of his stance or his stroke even for the shortest of Puts. And as to that Mashie shot, where you loft high over an abominable bunker and fall dead with a back spin and a cut to the right on a keen and declivitous green — is there any stroke in any game quite so delightfully difficult as that?

Not only is the stroke in golf an extremely difficult one, it is also an extremely complicated one, more especially the Drive, in which its principles are accentuated. It is in fact a subtle combination of a swing and a hit; the "hit" portion being deftly incorporated into the "swing" portion just as the head of the club reaches the ball, yet without disturbing the regular rhythm of the motion. The whole body must turn on the pivot of the head of the right thigh-bone working in the cotyloidal cavity of the *os innominatum* or nameless bone, the head, right knee, and right foot remaining fixed, with the eyes riveted on the ball. In the upward swing, the vertebral column rotates upon the head of the right femur, the right knee being fixed; but as the club-head nears the ball, the fulcrum is rapidly changed from the right to the left hip, the spine now rotating on the left thigh-bone, the left knee being fixed; and the velocity is accelerated by the arms and wrists, in order to add the force of the muscles to the weight of the body, thus gaining the greatest impetus possible. Not every professional instructor has succeeded in putting before his pupil this anatomical exposition of the correct stroke in golf. " Juist swoop her awa', maister," says one instructor. "*Hit* ut, mon," says another. Both are right, but such apparently discordant admonitions puzzle the neophyte. The professional also never wearies of telling you to "follow through"—almost the phrase has become a bye-word and a hissing on the links. But the "follow through" is merely evidence of three things: that you have poised the body properly; that you have swung correctly; and that you have "hit" at the moment of impact without destroying the rhythm; though probably the endeavour to "follow through" is an aid towards the correct accomplishment of these three things. The complexity of this movement is, I take it, one of the chiefest of the difficulties in golf, and the one hardest to be surmounted by the unyouthful novice. No stroke in any other game is quite like it; so that proficiency in other games is neither a criterion of, nor a preparation for, proficiency in golf.

One comfortable thing there is about golf: it does not need any excessive training. You need not reduce your weight, as you must for steeple-chasing; you need not be desperately careful about your wind, as you must be if you are entering for the half-mile or the mile. The heavy-weight and the light-weight are evenly matched on the links. Indeed an illustrious exponent of the game has said in print that it is as well that the golfer should pursue his ordinary mode of living, that he should make no extraordinary variation from his regular regimen. If he is accustomed to his pipe and his glass, well and good. So far so good. But there is this to be said. Golf above all things needs the steadiest of nerves, the clearest eye, and the most imperturbable of brains. If you are given to burning the midnight oil over books — or bridge, the odds will be against you on the links. Perhaps, as a matter of fact, golf is more exacting than a steeple-chase or the half-mile: it tries endurance; it tries the judgment; it tries the temper. No kind of sport sooner finds out a man's weak point than does golf. Two or three months will put you in trim for polo; golf demands the training of a lifetime. In golf this human machine of ours is put to the severest test; and if it has been overworked or abused, it is more than likely to break down between the teeing-ground and the green.

XV

YET not a little has been said, in a semi-sarcastic way, by devotees of other games than golf, about the comparative ease with which — as the sayers aver — a stationary ball can be, or should be, struck, as compared with one in motion. These detractors forget the nicety of the stroke that is required. A tennis-player has a whole court into which to play; a cricketer a whole field; the golfer has to put his ball into a hole of the size of a jam-pot, a quarter of a mile away. Indeed, the difficulties of golf are innumerable and incalculable. Take, for example, that simple rule, "keep your eye on the ball." It is unheard of in tennis; it is needless in cricket; in golf it is iterated and reiterated times without number — and infringed as often as repeated. Yet not everybody, I think, knows the reasons of the tendency to infringe it. One of them is this: As anatomists know, the crystalline lens in the eye automatically accommodates itself, by means of the ciliary muscle, to the focus of the object looked at. Now, many players get into the habit of looking intently at the flag, then suddenly reverting their gaze to their ball and striking before the lens has adapted itself to the new and nearer focus, with the result that they see the ball indistinctly and hit inaccurately. It is not that one does not *look* at one's ball; it is that one does not take time to look properly. To prove my theory, let anyone gaze steadfastly at a distant object and then quickly direct the eye to one close at one's foot. To learn that it requires time for the outlines of the latter to grow definite and distinct will be a lesson he will find invaluable on the links.

But indeed upon this all-important and fundamental rule, ''Keep your eye on the ball,'' there might be written, by him who had ability for the task, a whole Baconian essay, for in this rule is comprised all the law and the prophets. In itself this injunction seems simplicity itself;

to the practical carrying out thereof there are obstacles insuperable. I have touched on the difficulties incident to the focussing of the crystalline lens; yet these, compared with obstacles less obvious, are nearly negligible — at least to youth. To youth the focussing of the crystalline lens is happily not only automatic, but instantaneous; 't is age has to be patient and circumspect — in golf as in all things else: youth cuts the Gordian knot; age, poor age, saws through it. — But I digress. One of the chiefest impediments to a rigid observance of this the chiefest of rules lies in the fact that almost always the unpracticed golfer has an incontinent desire to see whither his ball is going before even he has hit it. The desire may be natural, but, without the shadow of a doubt, to indulge it is fatal. James Braid in his ''How to Play Golf'' has found for this desire an ingenious explanation. ''The fact seems to be,'' he says, ''that the mind, and the optic nerve through it, works rather more

quickly than the arms and the body.'' It may
.be so. This mind of man is a highly culpable
entity, and the optic nerve should have more
sense than to yield to its demands. Men have
I known, not a few, who resort to adventitious
aids by which to thwart its nefarious designs.
Only last week a golfer of repute, in the smoking-room of my club, frankly avowed that he
took a caddie, not so much for the purpose of
carrying his clubs, as because, when he had
a caddie, he was less apt to take his eye off
his ball. —How peccant, how very peccant,
human nature is! The mind of man, so it
seems, even when most intent on the most important business in hand, is so indisciplinable,
so incorrigible, so ungovernable by the owner
of that mind himself, that that owner has perforce artificially to avoid a temptation which
he feels he cannot resist.

Again, curiously enough, if you impress
upon yourself too anxiously this maxim call-
ing upon you to look at your ball, you will

find yourself deprived of the power to look at
it at all, as a man who tries to count his own
pulse unconsciously perturbs it. Your eye
wanders back and forth; you look at the top
of the abiding sphere; you look at its back;
often you look at your club instead of at your
ball. As a matter of fact, instead of *looking*,
you are *thinking;* and to *think*, when you
ought to *play*, is the madness of mania.

"What then," so do I imagine an irascible
reader to ejaculate, "what then the use of all
this learned descant on the Mystery of Golf,
and all these numerous attempts by tutors and
writers to elucidate for me the intricacies and
complexities of this abominable game, if I may
not on the links think upon and carry out their
lucubrations?"—I prithee give us grace.
Theorize not when you are playing in a match.
Theorize in your study, experiment when you
practise; but if you do not wish to go forth to
certain defeat—and of a surety to the taking
of your eye off your ball, cease you from theo-

rizing in a match. For, to think out a stroke implies diffidence in that stroke; and than diffidence there is not a more fatal foe to golf.

Howsoever, to sum up: until a man has learned to keep his eye on his ball, he will not play golf. He may be an excellent fellow; he may be the most jovial of companions, the sagest of counsellors, the truest of friends; but unless he can keep his eye on his ball never will he be a golfer.

Indeed, sometimes I am inclined to think that for a man invariably to be able to keep this one commandment, he must be *good;* that perhaps only the man who could keep the ten commandments could keep this one. For, mark you, it requires so many virtues, certainly that greatest of Tennyson his trinity, self-control. Not every good man will be a good golfer; but I challenge any one to dispute the fact that every really good golfer will at heart be a good man. Golf, in short, is not so much a game as it is a creed and a religion. Only the man who has not learned how thoroughly under control he must keep his mind, his body, and his morals, will dispute that assertion.—

I have said that art and sport are near akin. Are not art and sport and religion very nearly akin?

Besides, not every one knows the full significance of that simple verb "to look" in this simple but cardinal injunction. You must "look" with the most concentrated and absorbed attention. A casual or half-hearted look is suicidal. And you must look with the mind's eye as well as with the sensory one—and the one must be as keen, as clear, and as alert as the other.

XVI

THE difficulties of golf are immense. For think for a moment: there is scarcely a muscle in the body that is not called into play; and every muscle is controlled by a nerve. In fact, every muscle is a bundle of fibres or spindles, and every fibre or spindle is controlled by a branch of a nerve, cannot contract save in response to a stimulus conveyed to it by a branch of a nerve. Unless an order is sent from the brain and distributed to each and every part of the machinery which moves the trunk and limbs, not a movement can be made. And to ensure harmonious and coördinate movement, those orders must be very carefully, not only timed, but apportioned. Indeed, it would seem that duplicate orders, that two sets of stimuli, have to be despatched. There is, first, that which governs the "muscular sense," or, as some physiologists prefer to call it, the kinæsthesis, the sense that determines how tightly to hold the club and that poises the body for the swing. It is the sense, speaking generally, which ensures the proper relative rigidity or flexibility of opposing flexor and extensor muscles. It is chiefly concerned in judging distance, and is especially noticeable in the short Approach.

In the second place, there is the hit or swing.
This is the office of the motor centres, and is
brought about by a strong contraction of muscles, a contraction that should be rapidly yet
perfectly evenly increased. Both sets of stimuli
must be intimately and intricately combined
throughout the whole course of the swing : the
wrists must ease off at the top and tauten at
the end ; the left knee must be loose at the be-
ginning and firm at the finish ; and the change
from one to the other must be as deftly and
gently, yet swiftly wrought, as a crescendo
passage from pianissimo to fortissimo on a
fiddle.

XVII

Is it possible, from this physiological point of
view, to determine what is the fundamental
difference between a good player and a bad?
Can we say what it is makes a great golfer?
At first sight one is inclined to answer, As
well try to find out what makes a great gen-

eral, a great poet, or a great artist. Genius plays as large a part on the links as it does in life; and "genius," the dictionary says, "implies the possession of high and peculiar natural gifts which enable their possessor to reach his ends by a sort of intuitive power." However, leaving the genius out of view as beyond the reach of ordinary explanation, what is it that enables one man always to go round under eighty and another never? Well, for one thing, I suspect Imitation plays a large part in golf—as indeed it does in all life. Dr. Alfred Russel Wallace and Professor Poulton have pointed out its importance in biology, and Professor Yrjö Hirn its importance in art. Mimicry it is, probably—whatever in its ultimate analysis mimicry may be—which is at the bottom of all education; that by which we learn to talk no less than to golf. The youthful caddie probably picks up the game by sheer unconscious imitation, and his motor centres being highly docile, the correct golfing swing

[69]

comes to him with ease — as a child learns to
talk simply by hearing its parents. The man
who takes up golf at thirty or forty, when the
motor centres are by no means docile, and the
nerve currents have been for years accustomed
to flow in very different channels, — cricket
channels and tennis channels, — the elderly
beginner has to learn golf as a man learns a
new language, by accidence and prosody. If
he can imitate his professional, well and good,
but he will in all probability have also to apply
himself assiduously to the grammar of the
game. But to imitate requires the innervation
of nerve centres in the brain — all unconscious,
or rather all sub-conscious, as no doubt that
innervation is.

To begin at the bottom then, if the physiologists are not all wrong, to excel in golf requires
first of all a good brain. There is a part of the
brain called the corpora striata. ''The corpora striata,'' say the neurologists, '' are great
motor ganglia in some way concerned with

the execution of voluntary, emotional, and ideo-motor movements."[1] "The Corpus Striatum," says Broadbent, ". . . translates volitions into actions, or puts in execution the commands of the intellect; that is, it selects, so to speak, the motor nerve nuclei in the medulla and cord appropriate for the performance of the desired action, and sends down the impulses which set them in motion."[2] Nor is that all. In co-operation with the corpora striata is the cerebellum, which "co-ordinates movements . . . or combines the general movements . . . ordered by volition" (*Ib.*). —That is to say, if you want to move your arms and legs together *so*, you must call upon the striate bodies and the little brain to convey the orders; and if the *so* is a highly complicated and delicate series of movements, they must be good striate bodies and a good

[1] *The Brain as an Organ of Mind.* By H. Charlton Bastian, London, 1880, p. 564.

[2] *British Medical Journal*, April 1, 1876. Quoted by Bastian, *op. cit.*, p. 567.

little brain to be equal to it ; and to these un-
doubtedly we must add a good medulla and a
good spinal cord to boot.

Secondly, given a first-class corpus striatum and a cerebellum equally good, these two
parts of the brain, together with the cord and
all the nerve-cells and fibres by which they op-
erate, must be educated, by constant practice,
to perform smoothly, quickly, and forcibly the
complex motions necessary for the peculiar
stroke of golf. This, I take it, is done by what
Professor Loeb calls the "associative memory." The associative memory is a very important affair indeed. Loeb goes so far as to
make it synonymous with the will, with self-
consciousness, with the Ego! Yet its office
and function are simple, namely to ensure
the almost automatic sequence of such movements as have previously been deliberately
and hesitatingly combined. The golf stroke
is a highly complex one, and one necessitating
the innervation of innumerable cerebro-spinal

centres. Not only hand and eye, but arm, wrist, shoulders, back, loins, and legs must be stimulated to action. No wonder that the associative memory has to be most carefully cultivated in golf. To be able, without thinking about it, to take your stance, do your waggle, swing back, pause, come forward, hit hard, and follow through well over the left shoulder, always self-confidently—ah! this requires a first-class brain, a first-class spinal cord, and first-class muscles.

What the anatomists say is this, that, if the proper orders are issued from the cortex, and gathered up and distributed by the corpora striata and the cerebellum, are then transferred through the crus cerebri, the pons varolii, and the anterior pyramid of the medulla oblongata, down the lateral columns of the spinal cord into the anterior cornua of grey matter in the cervical, the dorsal, and the lumbar region, they will then "traverse the motor nerves at the rate of about a hundred and eleven feet a second and speedily excite definite groups of muscles in definite ways with the effect of producing the desired movements" (Bastian).

"Definite ways" and "desired movements" "speedily excited"! Gramercy! Are not these THE *desiderata* in golf?

But Bastian and Broadbent, I shall be told, are a bit out of date. Let me then quote Sherrington, a pre-eminent neurologist of the day. —Sherrington has tried to find out what it is that determines the final and definite movement of a set of muscles when more than one stimulus exists. His experiments were made on a dog. Would they had been made on a golfer, for if any one thing is patent to the indifferent golfer it is that he has to attend to a terrible lot of stimuli; and to which particular stimulus his muscles will respond he would give a great deal to know. (What duffer can tell beforehand whether he is going to slice or to pull, to baff or to top?) Sherrington, after a series of careful investigations argues thus: "The motor paths at any moment accord in a united pattern for harmonious synergy, coöperating for one effect. . . . The struggle between dissimilar arcs for mastery over their final common path takes place in the synaptic field at origin of the final neurones. . . . The issue of that conflict—namely, the determination of which competing arc shall for the time being reign over the final common path—is largely conditioned by three factors. One of these is the relative intensity of the stimulation. . . . A second main determinant . . . is the functional species of those reflexes. . . . A third main factor deciding the conflict between the competing reflexes is 'fatigue.'. . . The animal mechanism is thus given solidarity by this principle which for each effector organ allows and regulates interchange of the arcs playing upon it, a principle which I would briefly term that of 'the interaction of reflexes about their common path.'"" That is to say, muscles are moved by orders issued by the neurone or nerve centre governing those muscles; when this neurone receives conflicting orders from headquarters, it transmits only one, and this one is determined by (*a*) its strength; (*b*) its character; or (*c*) its freshness. Accordingly, the task for the golfer is by no means an easy one, for he has to move several sets of muscles, and he has to see to it that the orders issued to their respective neurones are strong, are of a particular character, and are fresh. If he does not know what sort of an order to issue: if, for instance, he forgets for the fractional part of a second, any one of the numerous injunctions imperative for a proper stroke —the firm grip, the eye on the ball, the head steady, the right foot fixed, the rhythmic backswing, the twirl of the wrists, the accelerated velocity, the hit at the impact, the glorious

---

[1] *Address to the Physiological Section of the British Association for the Advancement of Science, 1904.*

follow-through, to say nothing of the preliminary stance, waggle, judging of distance, and correct angle of feet, elbows, body, and whatnot — well, all I can say is that woe betides him. "The multiplicity of the conflict," says Sherrington, "seems extreme." We can positively assure him that it is.

I am afraid, however, that unless these learned anatomists and neurologists can also tell us some remedy for improperly issued and incorrectly communicated orders, I am afraid their lucubrations will be of no very great practical value to the golfer who is off his game. It would be a comfort to find cut what portion of the anatomical apparatus really was at fault. It would be a comfort to be able to fix the blame, say, on the infundibulum of the pituitary body or the valve of Vieussens. Which the offending centre is, I am afraid we shall not know till some foozling golfer submits to trepanning.— Perhaps not even then; for if, as I believe is the case, no alienist has yet been able to discover a

cerebral lesion in the lunatic, it is not likely
that the surgeon will find one in the foozler.

And yet it is always some unknown but
sinning centre that the erring golfer blames.
The bad workman used to complain of his
tools; but, with numberless tools to choose
from, and with absolute power of choice, the
bad golfer is perforce driven to complain of
some part of himself.—Never himself apparently.—The Old Adam dies hard. It is always one's digestion, or one's liver, or one's
suprarenal capsules that are at fault.—Which
is a curious ethico-psychological fact.—At all
events it is a tremendous compliment to the
fascination of golf that it is to these technical
adumbrations of the anatomist that we are
driven in order to explain or to excuse the vagaries of our game. One does not get "off"
one's football in this way, or one's chess or
one's poker or one's bridge; and if one did,
one would hardly go to neurology or to histo-
logical pathology for the cause.

XVIII

AND yet, what, after all, do these innumerable excuses that the poor golfer invents for himself after a bad round mean? Whom or what is he blaming? Is he not made up of cerebral and cerebellar centres; of cranial and spinal nerves; of neurones and synaptic fields; of extensor and flexor muscles? Are they not *he*? Which is the blamer and which is the blamed? Is there some inscrutable and immaterial psychic centre, inerrant and supreme, that sits enthroned aloft, and sways and rules these lesser centres? Shall we find in golf proof of the existence of a Soul?

Of a soul! If the physical mysteries of golf are so recondite, what of the psychic? These, I fear, be beyond us. How analyse the complexities of the human golfing soul? How tread the labyrinthine mazes of temperament and of character? How unravel the mesh-work of feelings and emotions, hopes and desires and fears, exultations and disappointments, heated angers, heavy despondencies; the wrath so hard to allay or ere the sun goes down; the vain imaginings, the ridiculous puffings-up of our little souls, of our silly little souls, over a hole halved in three or a circumvented stymie? Or how explain the disturbances these bring about in the higher layers, and the resulting delinquencies of the motor muscles?—In golf we see in its profoundest aspect that profound problem of the relation of mind to matter. Nowhere in the sum-total of the activities of life is this puzzle presented to us in acuter shape than on the links. Is there an ideal and immaterial Self in the golfer which knows precisely what it wants to do; and a bodily and fleshly one that will not or cannot carry out its behests? Is there an immaterial mind, superior to, but linked with, a material brain; or does the brain, in its subtlest interstices, shade off into an immaterial mind—a thing unimaginable by man? Does matter *think?* Are beef

[80]

and mutton and cabbage and potatoes transmuted into mind? —

We misuse words. We construct an artificial and needless barrier between mind and matter. By "matter" we simply mean something perceptible by our five senses; and by "mind" we simply mean something imperceptible by these senses. What "matter" really is we know as little as we do what "mind" really is. Suppose we had fifty senses; suppose we could actually perceive electricity, magnetism, æthereal vibrations, molecular motion, radial emanations, the interplay of emotion, the working of memory, the miracle of thought; suppose we could detect every and all of the myriad manifestations of energy as exhibited in the whole of this wonderful world! Would not the barrier be very hastily thrown down, and matter reveal itself as in reality one and the same with mind?

How extraordinarily limited is our conception of matter — so we call it! We say it has weight, colour, shape, sound, smell, texture, temperature, or taste—just seven or eight properties, just seven or eight (for "energy" is but a name for the unknown)! And every one of these is highly problematical, and even vanishes altogether under certain conditions: there is no weight at the centre of the earth; form and colour disappear in the dark; and all the rest go with paralysis or paresis. What if matter had six or seven hundred properties? What if mind had an infinite number of senses—or rather, what if mind required no senses for the perception of matter? Would not percipient mind and perceptible matter prove themselves identical; and perhaps the soul of man find itself coincident and conterminous with the Soul of the universe?

XIX

SPECULATIONS such as these carry us far. I seem to see in the conscientious golfer, doing his utmost, poor soul, to make matter (or mind) transcend its own powers, a type and symbol of mankind; of mankind warring with its environment, striving to overcome its limitations, reaching up to some unknown ideal, pressing towards some inscrutable goal. —What potentialities may not lurk in Man! If Amœba has developed into Man, into what may not Man develope! Some day we shall get some arch-angelical record rounds.—I wonder what Par Golf on the New Jerusalem links will be!—But these be transcendental themes.

One more speculative point, and we will drop metaphysics.—The golfer, strive as he may, is the slave of himself. Perhaps nothing is borne in upon the golfer more strongly after months of practice than that his place on the Club Handicap is determined by this his slavery to himself. There is not a golfer living but would say, "If I could, I would." The links prove the fatal and irrefragable chain of cause and effect. Every golfer *wills* to excel, and every golfer sedulously searches for the causes of failure.—'T is only one more proof of the transcendental identity of mind and matter. If, as the biologists aver, *omnis cellula e cellulâ*, and ratiocination and emotion are impossible without cells, surely then also *omnis idea ex ideâ*, and thought and volition are links in an interminable chain. . . .

XX

THE net-work of chains in the golfer's brain must be multitudinous. Golf seems to afford a corroboration of the theory that there are in man several layers of consciousness. Indeed, the late Mr. F. W. H. Myers might have found in golf a pertinent proof of the existence of his "subliminal self," to the functions of which he attributed so important a share. Why a man should, say in June, play a superlatively excellent game, and in July play an execrable one, in spite of the fact that he is in July just as fit as he was in June, that passes the wit of that man, poor wight! He broods over it; he almost weeps over it; he tries remedy after remedy, but in vain — beef and beer, total abstinence; a more elaborate waggle, no waggle; right foot foward, left foot firmer; a cigar before a game, no tobacco at all — all to no purpose. He knows to a nicety how every stroke should be played; but he is blessed, so he says, if he can play it. — Can it be that the so-called human "individual" is after all a duple, triple, quadruple, quintuple, or multiple personality? Almost it would seem so. You take your stance at the first tee, and Personality No. I severely makes up his mind to play carefully and well. At the approach, Personality No. II presses. At the put, Personality No. III is over-anxious, and is short. At the second tee, Personality No. IV flings care to the four winds of heaven. No. V takes his eye off the ball. No. VI goes into a bunker.

No. n swears (let us hope sub-liminally). By this time the exasperated golfer compares himself to the Gadarene demoniac.

Indeed, a veritable demon seems to enter into a man on the links. Otherwise what on earth possesses him that he should transgress the most elementary and the most easily obeyed of rules? Why should he take his eye off his ball? Why should he "press" or hurry his stroke? There lies his ball awaiting his pleasure, and would await it for a fortnight, for that matter — there is not even a time-limit for the address; and every spectator, by the stern etiquette of the game, is in duty bound to stand mute and patient the while he prepares to strike. What on earth possesses him that he should look up before he strikes or strike in a hurry? And yet man after man spoils stroke upon stroke by these infantine follies — and, worse and worse, spoils them consecutively! There is no physical or artificial impediment whatsoever.

Some ninety or a hundred yards of level turf lie between ball and hole. A club precisely made to suit that particular shot is handed you. Time and time again you have been taught exactly how to stand, exactly how to swing. And yet how often it has taken three, four, and even five strokes to cover those hundred yards! It would be laughable were it not so humiliating. In fact the impudent spectator does laugh — until he tries it himself; then, ah! then, he too gets a glimpse into that miracle of miracles, the human mind, which at one and the same time wills to do a thing and fails to do it; which knows precisely and could repeat by rote the exact means by which it is to be accomplished, yet is impotent to put them in force. And the means are so simple, so insanely simple. We need not be surprised that the impudent spectator does not even affect to conceal his laughter in his sleeve. — But neither need we be surprised that the experts, the adepts, those who have gone

through the humiliation of failure, watching
these puerilities from the veranda, are moved
rather to wonder than to laughter. They have
had more glimpses into the profundities and
complexities of the erring golfing mind than
they care to reckon, and they know that the
secret of this extraordinary and baffling conflict of mind and matter is a psychological
problem beyond the reach of physiology and
ontology combined.

XXI

TALK as neurologists and psychologists may,
what this fearfully and wonderfully made
thing called "mind" is we have not the re-
motest conception. *Five* layers of consciousness? Why, there is a whole civic community
underneath each one of us his hat or her bon-
net. Trained watchmen sit at eye-gate and
ear-gate and touch-gate and smell-gate and
taste-gate, and report to the Mayor and Al-

dermen of Mansoul regarding all personages who demand admission. Go on board ship, and not until the watchmen have assured themselves that the sound and vibration of the screw are harmless, will they let the city sleep, though the central council argue never so hard. Let the screw stop at the end of the voyage, and immediately the watchmen rouse the whole city, shouting that something has gone wrong. And, if the encephalon is a municipality, the bodily frame is, as it were, a whole nation under its government, whence, according to reports received from the portals, orders are issued for the mobilization of forces and the undertaking of huge campaigns — one battalion of muscles holding the legs in firm position; another sending the arms flying in all directions. And — mystery of mysteries, miracle among things miraculous — not only are there guards and officials and troops, but apparently there is a Generalissimo or an Emperor, who can look on and

analyse and criticise the doings and functions
of this nation and capital — can actually try
to discover the method of its own working and
put down in black and white the provisions
of its own constitution; for surely, reader,
this is precisely what you and I are attempting to do at this moment! The mind itself, so
it seems, can turn round upon itself, get out-
side of itself, and examine its own workings!
What a stupendous puzzle! Ah! there must
be more in the human mind than watchmen
and aldermen and mayor; there must be
lords spiritual as well as temporal — perhaps
a shrine and altar, and, behind a veil, a Holy
of Holies. In microcosmic Mind I seem to see
in miniature a tiny facsimile or homologue of
macrocosmic Spirit, that Spirit which not
only externalizes itself in Nature, but, as Plo-
tinus of Lycopolis hath it, "possesses sight
and knowledge of itself" (*apud* Tennemann).

But alas! how often the little microcosm
goes wrong! How desperately ignorant it is

of itself! — Well, few things bring home to
us better the depths of this our ignorance of
ourselves than its vagaries and eccentricities
on the links. What particular giant-cell in the
cortex of the brain fails to act when we take our
eye off our ball? Will any electrode teach us
that? And what cortical monitor indignantly
upbraids that cell immediately afterwards?
Will any theory of "multiple personality"
explain for us that? Constantly one part of
the mind takes another to task for dereliction
of duty. Cannot the mind see to it that the
municipality as a whole and the nation under
its rule act in unison? Can it be that there is
going on in each individual human being a
gigantic constitutional struggle exactly analo-
gous to that which is going on and has ever
been going on in every nation upon this ter-
rene periphery — a struggle to determine who
shall rule, what powers the ruler shall have,
and how his actions may be checked? So it
would seem. —

[91]

Looked at nearly, golf does, indeed, raise for our consideration deep and curious questions. But golf cannot answer them, any more than can the neurologists or the psychologists —or, for the matter of that, the constitutional historians. For in golf, so it would appear, the political constitution of this little human individual community is put to the severest and utmost test. So extremely complex, requiring the harmonious coöperation of so many sets of forces, is the task imposed by golf, that the whole body politic is thrown, every time it sets out on a round, into the throes of a constitutional crisis. A huge and difficult political problem suddenly confronts it, a problem for the correct solution of which the nation must act harmoniously and as a unit. The Republic is in danger, and the inhabitants rush about looking for one whom to appoint as Dictator.— *Or*, as the French say, well for that man among whose myriad cell-population there is always a Cincinnatus ready

to leave his plough and *attend to the game!*
for unless there is, there will be consternation
in the capital, and no concerted action, but
only vague hurryings and recriminations, and
rushings to and fro of disorderly mobs. But
alas! Cincinnati are rare, very, very rare. It
takes a great national cataclysm to throw up
a great leader of men. Only, indeed, in great
cataclysms are great men thrown up. What
an upheaval produced a Napoleon, what a
revolution a Washington! Ordinary events do
not produce extraordinary men. — Perhaps
this is why an extraordinary round can be
performed only by an extraordinary player.

What exasperates the ordinary man about
golf is that it seems to be a game utterly and
absolutely unamenable to reason. You may
speculate in stocks; you may lay odds on a
horse-race; but the money-market and the
turf are child's play compared with the un-
certainties of golf; — and this in spite of
the fact that, though you cannot control the

market, and know your horse only by hearsay, on the links it is on your own individual efforts that you count. My opponent to-day had had a bad night; so he dolefully told me, and expected defeat. What was the result? His record round for his links!—No; golf is not amenable to reason.—And here we find another factor in the extraordinary fascination of the game.—The unknown, says Tacitus, is always the wondered at. Well, metaphysics, golf, and the feminine heart will be wondered at long.—But from a search for the causes of the uniqueness of golf, we have been led into devious paths, indeed. Return we to the former.—

XXII

THAT golf is a game unique, need be proved to no golfer. He knows it only too well—often to his cost. "Are you playing this autumn?" I asked the other day of a stalwart jurisprudent—and jurisprudents, I take it, are among

the sanest and coolest-headed of men. "No;
I dare not," was his reply; "golf with me is
a disease, and I am too busy to play"; and
the answer raised not even a smile among the
smoking-room audience of the Club — which
fact, perhaps, was as significant as the reply.
"Golf to me," said another lover of the game,
"means health, strength, energy, and ambition"; and I trow not but that he meant these
beneficial properties extended far beyond the
links.

And, with the possible exception of Pa-
tience, is there any other game which one
can play all by one's self with so much enjoy-
ment? The Duffer can invent for himself a
nice, fat, easy-going, corpulent Colonel of, say,
an average of six per hole as his antagonist;
men high up in the handicap have always
Bogey; scratch men can compete with Par;
and it is always open to those happy gentle-
men who stand at "plus" to construct for
themselves a Colonel, lean of girth, keen in

skill, and as austere and severe as they like. Golf is a curious, to some a dangerous, game. If its lure once gets into the blood, it is nearly as difficult to cure as cancer.

"Well, I have been thinking about it," said a disconsolate friend to me the other day —he had strained his arm by too much play and was interdicted the links for a month by his doctor; "I have been thinking over it, and I dare say I shall find something else to do."—He did: he spent three hours daily in practising putting.—"I wonder if you would ever have married me, if you had taken up golf before you proposed," said a wife once. —It is related, too, of a famous Anglican Divine—a Doctor of Divinity (and I think this story is not quite a chestnut)—that, having come under the spell of the sport, in a burst of unecclesiastical frankness he confided to a friend that there was that in the game which made him forget his wife, his family, his country, and his God.

XXIII

Is this uniqueness explicable? Well, perhaps in no other game, for one thing, are you obliged, or have you time, so intensely to concentrate your every faculty on your every stroke. In no other game have you so to be master of yourself, as it were, to steady your-self,—your muscles, your nerves, your brain, nay, your mood, and your temper,—or to be master of yourself for so long a stretch. Four or five score strokes must be made, some of them with the strength of a sledge-hammer, many of them with the delicacy of a micro-tome, all of them with the precision of a ma-chine; and so to subdue this unruly body of ours, with its mobile muscles, its ebul-lient blood, its unquiet nerves, its perturbable brain, as to achieve that feat . . . one has to pass through much tribulation or ere that feat is even approximately achieved. In no other game are you left so desperately alone. In no other game does all depend upon your individual effort. There is nothing to hamper you, nothing to hinder you, nothing to hurry you.

Golf is so deliberate that the mind has ample time in which to act — another feature which differentiates it from other sports. In fact, the difference between a rapid game like tennis and a deliberate game like golf is similar to the difference between playing a piece of music with which you are familiar and reading note by note a piece of music that is new. In the one the fingers move spontaneously; in the other they are guided at every step by the brain. In no game, too, does so much depend upon a single stroke. In a three-days' cricket match tens of thousands of hits must be made; in three sets out of five in tennis certainly tens of hundreds; in the most important of matches in golf never so many as a couple of hundred; the intrinsic and proportionate importance of each hit being thus correspondingly increased. Nor in any other game are the conditions so fixed and invariable. In tennis, cricket, polo, racquets, the conditions change momentarily; before you have time to think, you have to strike at a ball coming at a different angle and with a different velocity and with a different cut from those of the one before; and you must strike it with a corresponding difference of angle, force, and cut. In every game, too, your opponent's skill may change. In golf there is one thing to be done, and only one: to put a stationary ball into a stationary hole. And to do that one thing depends entirely upon yourself. Perhaps it is because you, and you alone, are to blame if you miss it, that you feel so keenly, so intensely, a fumbled stroke —another proof of the uniqueness of the game. To make a duck's egg at cricket is provoking enough. To lose one's queen at chess is depressing; though one always hopes to make up for it by phænomenal play with the rooks. To go into the net at tennis is disappointing, but the disappointment is apt to wear off with the rapidity of the set. To foozle at golf—how it *hurts!* I have seen my little caddie turn away, not in anger, nor in contempt, nor in reproach, but in pity. As to a multiplicity of foozles! pity the friends—and the foes—and the family—of that man who makes them, of all men most deject and wretched!

XXIV

How golf bewrays the character! You may know a man for years, yet discover new traits in him on the links. Characteristics long buried beneath convention are suddenly resuscitated; foibles sedulously suppressed spring into existence; hereditary instincts lying dormant reveal themselves. I was once for the first time made aware of the Hibernian origin of a partner by his antics over an astonishing put which won him the hole: for a moment of time his club might have been a

shillelah, his feet moved to a jig. Golf brings
out idiosyncrasies and peculiarities. Sometimes it brings out more than these! Hence,
perhaps, the innumerability of the anecdotes
anent the irrepressibility of profanity while
playing the game—a game proverbially pro-
vocative of reprehensible expletives. My eyes
were lately opened to this sinister peculiarity
when playing with a man, the author of a
ponderous work, noted for the precision, even
for the purism, of his diction. Usually he
spake as he wrote, and he wrote for gentle-
men learned in the law. To my astonish-
ment, one afternoon, far away in the windle
straws on my right (we had diverged at the
tee), proceeded from him the deepest and
most earnest consignments to perdition of . . .
whether it was himself, or his ball, or his iron,
or the sum total of created things I did not dis-
tinctly understand. Not even had he a caddie
in whose hearing to ejaculate. It was in the
face of pure untainted Nature that he swore;

and his deliberate damns sounded like bolts
from the blue. Still, they comforted me.
They proved to me, the duffer, that to take a
foozle philosophically was not to be expected
of mortal man. Almost, I begin to think, a
false stroke in golf is more keenly felt than is
a rejected proposal. The girl may change her
mind, but a foozle is an irrevocable foozle, and
a hole lost is lost forever. The inexorability
of the game is appalling, and may well un-
nerve the timorous player. Nothing in the
rules of life and conduct is quite so rigid as
are the conditions of this simple-seeming so-
called "game." A hasty word may be re-
called, a miscalculation corrected, a blunder
apologized for; but to no man is it given con-
fidently to be able to say that he shall make
up for a missed approach by a super-magnifi-
cent put. Master as a man is of his muscles,
on the links too often they seem the sport of
chance. He may do his utmost; exert himself
to the sublimest limit of his ability; be cau-

tious as a cat, alert as the lynx, and yet fail
to place a simple round ball within three feet
of a simple round hole, when only an easily
computable number of paltry yards separate
one from other. To no one is it given to say,
"I shall play the next stroke well." That is
curious. If one makes up one's mind to it,
and is not thwarted, one can do most things
well. How is it that the utmost deliberation,
the extremest caution, the most scrupulous
care, will often fail to put you where you
would be? Almost it would seem that in golf
is required that thing called amongst men
"genius." One could no more undertake to
produce a perfect put at every attempt than
one could undertake to produce a perfect
poem. Perhaps this is why the great masters
of the art are held in such high esteem, an es-
timation never quite equalled by that accorded
to their fellow-champions in, say, cricket or
football. These are not, to my knowledge,
asked by enterprising publishers to pose for

their stance, or to supply photographs of their
attitudes, or to give diagrammatic illustrations, drawn to scale, of their legs and arms.
No; perhaps one of the profoundest secrets
of the profound fascination exercised by golf
lies in this, that, in spite of the fact that no
one may thwart, oppose, or impede, there is
no golfer living who could with surety assert
that he will positively always do any particular hole in any particular number of strokes.
Therein lies the irony of golf. The planets
move in orbits exact as mathematics itself.
The great balls of the universe are holed-out
year by year with a precision which mocks
our finest tools. Predict we can to the fraction
of a second when Venus will approach the
rim of the Sun, or Luna fall into the shadow
of the Earth. But man, the master-mechanic
of this terrestrial globe, versed in all the laws
of parabola and ellipse, can no more govern
the flight of his pigmy gutty than he can govern the flight of the summer swallow.

XXV

GOLF is unique, too, in that it can be played anywhere—on lone sea-shores or crowded heaths, over high-road and hedge, amid moss and weed, on the veldt, on the prairie, on the mead. (Obstacles are but "bunkers" to golf; the more the merrier. How encomiastic the St. Andrews golfer grows over his bunkers!) Certain links I know, far away on a western continent, a nine-hole course, miles from train or tram. Club-house there is none; you throw your covert coat and your hat over a fence and —play. There are no greens, there are no flags: the player more familiar with the ground goes ahead and gives you the line. The teeing-grounds are marked by the spots where the soil has been scraped by the boot for the where-withal for tees. Bunkers abound, and bad lies, in the form of hoof-marks and cart-ruts, do much more abound. Sheep and kine roam over them at will. For cooling drink after a heating round, you knock at a farm-house door for water. Yet to these links — and they are beautiful: high, hilly, green, a waving corn-field to your right, rolling pasture to your left, here and there a nodding coppice, and somnolent valleys variegating the scene — to these links daily gaily trudge ardent golfers, carrying clubs under a sub-arctic August sun — proof enough for me of the uniqueness of the game.

XXVI

AND yet it must be confessed that if this enthusiasm for the game were to be evoked in youths of sixteen or eighteen, and were strong enough to tempt them to forsake the crease or the goal for the links, not every one would applaud the lure. Not every one would be willing to see the youth of the United Kingdom of Great Britain and Ireland, or of the United States of America give up their national and traditional games. But there is no likelihood

of such a catastrophe. For high spirits and
supple joints golf is too sedate. Enthusiasts
will play it world without end, as they have
played it from time immemorial. And so, perhaps, will spirits that are losing the buoyancy
and joints that are losing the suppleness of
youth. But for the masses, golf to-day is a
fashion, as much as was tennis a few years
ago. To some this will be a hard saying, to
others a consolatory one. The thought that
his favourite links will some day be not so
infested will perhaps give the confirmed and
splenetic golfer heart of grace; the thought
that his revered pass-time should be subject
to fashion will wring from the confirmed and
unsplenetic golfer hearty dissent. Yet that
golf is a passing fashion I venture to assert.
Cheap balls and iron clubs have put it within
the reach of the many. And the many, being
usually a body of workers by hand or brain,
with only so much money, time, and energy
at their disposal, find in this not-too-violent

exercise a recreation suited to their limitations. In golf, too, you require only a single partner, not a team; a match can be arranged by telephone in five minutes, and can be finished between office-hours and dinner-time. But when the links become a moving multitude resonant with "'Fores!'" when severe competition raises record scores to a point which will kill ambition in the novice and the amateur; when 'Arry and 'Arriet take to afternoon foursomes—as before long they will; why, then it is probable that the many who are not 'Arrys and 'Arriets will look about them for less popular sports. All games, saving only those national and traditional, have their day; as witness: first, archery, then croquet, then tennis, and now golf. Within the precincts of St. Andrews all this will be heresy. But St. Andrews will outlast fashion, as certainly it preceded fashion. Nor, I take it, would St. Andrews murmur if the popular fashion for golf did some day wane!

How many balls already simultaneously encumber that classic ground? But all this very little concerns us here. Golf is in the very infancy of fashion, and will outlast many a generation yet.

What may take the place of golf when it ceases to be a fashion, it is hard to say. Archery, croquet, tennis, will never come in again. The bicycle is now an economic vehicle. Bowling-on-the-green is daily drawing devotees; but it cannot rival golf. Lacrosse is for the agile. Polo is expensive; so would be falconry. The dirigibility of the balloon is still a very long way off, in spite of MM. Maxim and Santos-Dumont; and at present not every one can afford to run the risk of being dumped five hundred miles from home. Aviation by aeroplanes is for the few. Horse-racing and yachting are for kings or millionaires. Fencing is for the leisured and the cultured. Perhaps, when motor-cars come within measureable distance of possessivity, and roads are made, as Mr. H. G. Wells would have them, sensibly broad, we may see some startling sport. Speed is a tremendous intoxicant. When 'Arry can 'ire a heighty-'orsepower hauto, there will be fun —for 'Arry.—But were I to hazard a conjecture, I should be inclined to prophesy a wonderful future for rifle-practice. The weapon is comparatively cheap, so is the ammunition; Morris-tubes and sub-targets are easily erected, and ranges and butts ought to be as obtainable as links. Already rifle-clubs abound, and proficiency in musketry is yearly more highly esteemed—some twenty thousand people turned out to welcome home the King's Prizeman of 1904.

XXVII

But at the present moment golf is certainly as fashionable as unique, if we regard the mass of theoretical instruction proffered to the public, purporting to teach them how it should be played. Books, magazines, illustrations, photographs, diagrams, mathematical formulæ, algebraic symbols, and rules without number, appear monthly. The swing, the stance, the address, the waggle—all are solemnly descanted upon. Why? Probably the true answer to this little question is as disingenuous as it will be disappointing. Cricket, football, tennis, racquets, and the rest, despite the adjectives "royal" and "ancient," are, to the masses, old; they were played by thousands long before the modern craze for scientific accuracy and analysis seized upon theoretic exponents of sport. Golf to the masses is comparatively new. Golf has been taken up by grey heads and stiff joints. And stiff joints and grey heads, unaccustomed to the swing proper to drivers and cleeks, require theoretic instruction. An eminent player and elucidator of the game, expatiating on the multiplicity of the coexisting styles of play,

looks forward to the time when some more
rigid and scientific analysis of stroke shall be
possible, and when some fixed and ideal form
shall be evolved. Personally, I look forward to
the time when all these elaborate directions as
to the precise manner in which some twenty-
seven and a half drachms avoirdupois of
gutta-percha shall be propelled some two hundred yards shall be regarded as a curious
characteristic of a bygone age. Some two
thousand years ago Aristotle had the temerity
to affirm that the lyre was learned by playing
the lyre. Some two thousand years hence
some golfer may have the temerity to affirm
that golf is learned by playing golf. In proof
of which rash assertion I here adduce an illus-
tration as simple and as disappointing as, I
feel, is my prediction. There is at my club
a little caddie, by name Willie Dobson (note
the name, I pray you; it may some day be inscribed on as many clubs as is now the name
of Willie Dunn). Willie Dobson just now

weighs between five and six stone, measures about four foot two, and is aged *circiter* thirteen years. He has not read Mr. Horace Hutchinson or William Parkes, junior, or Herd, or Mr. Low, or Mr. Beldam; he knows not the Badminton Series; he is all unaware that Vardon and Braid have become scribes as well as champions of the game; he has not heard of ''advanced golf''; he has not studied instantaneous photographs of distinguished drivers, approachers, and putters; and I seriously doubt whether he has practiced before a mirror. The Bogey for my links, as computed by a careful committee for grown-up men, is eighty-one. Well, Willie has done them in eighty-five, and can do them again. Half a century hence he will be asked to write a book on golf. Would I could read it! — To conclude. Did we all commence golf as Willie Dobson has commenced it, there would be little need of rule or rote. Willie Dobson learned golf by caddying for a St. Andrews golfer.

Not but that, I am fully prepared to admit, there is absolute necessity for commencing the game properly. Perhaps another feature in the uniqueness of golf is that, in it, style counts for so much, so very much. So long as you play with a straight bat you may run up a score at cricket with a poor style; but already in golf I have met men who, by some unaccountable trick of style, had so far got out of the particular knack of the drive, that they had perforce to tee off with a cleek. How many beginners, too, are "off" their irons to-day and "off" their wooden clubs to-morrow! However, I take it these mishaps occur rather to the grey-headed and stiff-jointed beginners than to Willie Dobsons or Willie Dunns; although W. Fernie's lamentable performance at Prestwich, in 1887, is a warning even to the expert. Up almost to the days of the championship match, we are told, he was playing in perfect form; during the contest he heeled ball after ball.

[114]

XXVIII

FEW things shew so clearly the influence of
the mind upon the body as the game of golf.
The links, I have sometimes thought, might
not seldom with advantage be exchanged for
the laboratory by both professors and students of experimental psychology. For example, I have it on very direct evidence,
namely, from one of the contestants himself,
that one of the greatest matches in the history
of golf was in all probability decided on psychological grounds alone. Between the oppo-
nents there was little, if any, disparity of skill;
but one had the advantage of strength and
experience. By means of the first qualification
he again and again outdrove his antagonist;
by means of the second he retained un-
shaken, throughout the five days' arduous
struggle, his judgment and his nerve. The
consequence was, so more than one spectator averred, that the younger adversary was

tempted to "press"; and the inevitable and
fatal consequence of pressing was loss of accuracy and ultimate defeat. How many golfers, too, either resent or welcome the existence
of a "gallery." If there is nothing in golf but
a test of strength and skill, what should matter
the presence or the absence of some few score
on-looking human folk? What cricketer at
Lord's or the Oval gives a thought to the Pa-
vilion? Yet some men a gallery disconcerts,
others it stimulates. Assuredly this influence
is psychic. The fact is that the judgment and
the delicacy requisite in golf are so extreme,
so fine, that the minutest perturbation of the
mind, and therefore of the brain, and therefore of the whole nervous system by which
the action of the muscles is controlled, affects
the accuracy of the stroke. It would be interesting to attach sphygmographs to various
golfers, both phlegmatic and mercurial, and
to compare the tracings under the varying
conditions of the game, — though probably

even the pulse-beats are a less delicate criterion of mental equanimity or perturbation than are the drive, the approach, and the put. A famous Italian experimental psychologist, by name Angelo Mosso, has recently proved, by means of a nicely balanced instrument, that each and every varying condition of the mind produces a corresponding variation in the circulation of the blood. Just such another nicely balanced instrument is golf. (Was it not a famous — or an infamous — golfer who was once upset by the singing of a da . . . of a dastardly lark?) The merest tyro soon discovers something of this. Perhaps this is why the tyro is so particular to enquire as to what he should eat and what he should drink and how-withal he should be clothed. —

To the on-looker these minutiæ are, of course, highly amusing. But the amused on-looker little knows on what minute things great golfing matters sometimes turn. There is a fatefulness about golf that is terrorizing.

Momentous events often enough hang upon
the minutest causes. But nothing even in the
realm of the physical sciences is more inexorable or rigid than golf. The centre of gravity
of the solid earth, so they tell us, is altered
by a footstep. That is conceivable, though it
is not perceptible. Yet with my own eyes have
I seen a great match between two rival clubs,
with twenty players a side, determined by a
two-foot put missed at the eighteenth hole.
And did not Alexander Herd, in that extraordinary tournament of the Professional Golfers' Association on the Mid-Surrey links, at
Richmond Old Deer-Park, in 1904, just
fail of actually defeating Braid, Vardon, and
Taylor in succession, by a less than two-foot
put missed at the seventeenth hole? I have
known a club championship to depend upon
a stymie at the nineteenth hole. "What will
you give us?" said once one pair in a foursome to the other. "O, a stroke on the nineteenth hole," was the jocular reply. By that

stroke, by the grimness of fate, that match was decided. — The veteran golfer thinks on these things and ponders them in his heart; and little he recks of the amusement or the derision of the on-looker. *Mathematica mathematicis scribuntur.*

It may be that the recital of such mistakes as these, made by eminent golfers, is, on the whole, somewhat of a consolation to the duffer, to him to whom, for the time being, golf seems little more than a series of mistakes. And so it may be. And the recital might be abundantly amplified. The champion of a hemisphere once missed the winning of a pewter by taking eleven for a hundred-and-seventy-five-yard hole in which no bunker intervened between teeing ground and putting green; a hole which he usually accomplished in three, sometimes in two.[1] And I

[1] It should be told, however, that the course was extremely narrow, and that a horrible ravine skirted the green. The player in question drove out of bounds twice, and then into the horrible ravine.

once saw one of the most expert of lady golfers, when playing against the lady champion
of a great colony, land twice in succession in
a water-jump in making a thirty-yard approach, when the lie was perfect, she was
three feet from the stream, and the ground
was flat! — Yes, such things are consoling to
us all. To err is human, even on the links.

I have sometimes thought, too, that I could
detect a curious psychic contagion on the
links. It is within every golfer's experience
that he finds he plays well against certain op-
ponents and badly against others; and this,
not so much on account of the quality of his
opponent's game as on account of his temperament or character. You are steadied by
one man, you are upset by another; this opponent hurries you and harries you, the other
unwittingly calls out your better self. This is
highly curious — and highly significant, being indeed one more proof of the fact that
in this game, which outwardly and to the in-

experienced seems merely a test of skill and
strength, there is in reality some unimaginable and unsearchable contest between some
inner and innominable centres in the com-
batants. For it is not his mere trick of
manner that makes one man antipathetic to
another on the links; it is something far more
deep-seated than this: it is something inher-
ent in the innermost recesses of his nature,
something intangible, invisible, arcanal. —
Is there some inscrutable medium between
soul and soul, the existence of which only
golf reveals? I recommend the links as a fruitful field for the experiments of the thought-
reader, or the investigations of the Society for
Psychical Research.

XXIX

GOLF, indeed, is a fruitful field of psychological phænomena. For example, hypnotists of
the most modern school aver, I believe, that

there exist somewhere in the brain or mind of
man five distinct layers of consciousness. For
proofs of multiple consciousness the hypno-
tist should frequent the links. He will there
often find one layer of consciousness roundly
upbraiding another, sometimes in the most
violent language of abuse, for a foozled
stroke; and so earnest sometimes is the vitu-
peration poured by the unmerciful abuser
upon the unfortunate foozler, that truly one
is apt sometimes sincerely to commiserate
the former, and to regard him as the victim
of a multiple personality, and not at all blame-
able for his own poor play. Golfers, too, have
I known who imagine themselves constantly
accompanied by a sort of Socratic *daimon*
prompting them to this, that, or the other
method of manipulating the club—without
doubt a mystic manner of looking upon one's
alter ego. It would be interesting to "suggest" to a duffer, while in the cataleptic
trance, to keep his eye on the ball, and to fol-

low through, and then to watch the result. If these fundamental rules (so easy to preach, so difficult to practice) could be relegated to some automatic sub-stratum of consciousness, leaving the higher centres free to judge of distance and direction (for it is thus, probably, that the man who has golfed from childhood plays), the task of many a professional might be simplified. All of which goes to show that, in the game of golf, the mind plays a larger part than, in many quarters, is apt to be imagined.

The physiological explanation of the prepondering influence of mind over body in golf is this: Precise coördination of hand and eye is necessary; this coördination is directed by nerve currents (cerebral and cerebro-spinal) conveyed to the muscles; which nerve-currents depend for their regularity upon the mind. Unless the supreme and regulating centres of intelligence, wherein lie imbedded the cells from which orders for muscular move-

ment derive, are, first, in thorough working
order, and, second, intent upon the business
in hand, the orders conveyed through the
delicate efferent nerve-fibres governing the
equally delicate muscular fibres of the fingers,
hands, wrists, legs, and arms, will be inef-
fectual, and the resulting stroke inaccurate.
In short it would seem that a man, to play
golf well, must play like a machine; but like
a machine in which the mental motor must
be as perfect as the muscular mechanism.

XXX

PERHAPS the sense most prominently brought
into play in golf is that to which I have already
referred and which is known to physiologists
as kinæsthesis or the "muscular sense"—
the sixth sense, as it is sometimes called. By
the muscular sense it is that we calculate the
exact amount of force required for a particular posture or movement. It is by this sense

that we wield so deftly the knife and fork, the spoon, and the pen. To keep a bouncing ball bouncing just so high, requires just such a tap and no more. That tap is regulated by the muscular sense. To poise an ounce weight on the tips of the fingers requires just such relative rigidity of the phalangeal flexors and extensors. Double the resilience of the bouncing-ball, or poise two ounces instead of one, and the taps or the muscular rigidity must immediately be changed, the amount of change being regulated by the muscular sense. Now, in ordinary life this sense is exercised only within very narrow limits, and is rarely, if ever, called upon to judge of great distances. It carries food to the mouth; it raises a hat; it is skilled in

" The nice conduct of a clouded cane ";

it may occasionally throw a stone at a dog or a boot-jack at a cat; but it does little more. Some games exercise it more than others. In cricket it is highly valuable; in tennis and racquets even more so. Rowing utilizes it but little. In baseball you hit, and in football you kick, as hard as you can. In croquet it is important. But in croquet all the strokes are the same. But in golf! In golf, within the space of ten minutes, it is called upon to drive two hundred yards; loft another hundred; and put five inches. In golf you have strokes that require the strength of a slog in cricket, combined with the delicacy of cup-and-ball. In golf you get the whole gamut of the muscular sense, from the gigantic swipe at the tee to the gentle tap on the green. It is called into play at every stroke, and it differs with every difference of club—its weight, its length of shaft, the angle which its face subtends to the horizon, its rigidity or flexibility, the construction and material of its head.—Golf, in short, is a sort of Gargantuan jugglery, a prodigious prestidigitation, a Titanic thimble-rigging, a mighty legerdemain.

XXXI

Among the psychological aspects of golf is its effect upon the character; and this is neither small nor unimportant. There is no more inexorable an opponent than your links. Implacable as fate, they exact to the uttermost farthing for the minutest divergence from the narrow path. Atropos will sooner be turned aside than they. Your mortal foe may relent, may show mercy; in golf, between first tee and home hole look thou not for changeableness nor shadow of turning. And for peccant man this is good. It is disciplinary. Whom golf loveth it chasteneth; and few men but come off the course, be it on the first round or the five-hundredth, chastened, and by consequence strengthened. Even victory fails to puff up, for victory always is hardly won, and always it is not your natural, but your human, foe that is defeated. Your natural foe, with his hazards and his bunkers still unharmed

[127]

and threatening, still grimly smiles, still challenges you to completer conquest. For, in short, your links are invincible. Could you hole out in one on every drive the holes would be only halved, and you and they would come out but even all. For *space* is the one eternal and immutable enemy of man. It is to conquer space that we resort to steam and electricity, the penny-post and the tram-car, the motor and the bicycle, the brassey, the cleek. So that, even if you brought every hole within holing distance of every drive, the necessity of that drive would prove the necessity of that effort to overcome space. It would be an attractive, but perhaps a too transcendental, thought to imagine that in some future, supra-lunary, n-dimensional world, this infinite enemy, space, will at last be worsted. There the teeing-ground will be identical with the putting-green, the drive one with the put, the hole coincident with the tee. There achievement will be accomplished without effort, attainment will be identical with endeavour, the ideal will be the real. That will be on beatific links indeed, where room for bunkers will be none.

XXXII

FOR not even against Bogey is it that even on this spatial and temporal world you pit your strength. Bogey is but a human compromise between erring man and unerring Nature; an ideal player, an apotheosized golfer, an anthropomorphic deity of the links. Bogey is that great exemplar whom, despairing of overcoming great Nature herself, we each strive to imitate, even to excel. He is the player who is never off his game; is always in training; never makes a mistake; never loses his temper or his head; whom no defeat dejects and no victory elates; who is imperturbable, persistent, placid. In golf, as in life, frail and mortal man is brought into conflict with sempiternal Nature. His pigmy strength, his uncertain skill, are arrayed against the immutable, the inexpugnable. And as we may say that all evolution, all progress, all development have come about solely because of unceasing combat with unyielding Nature; that man is not now an ape, and the ape is not now a mollusc, because of that fight with cosmic force; so we may see in golf something of the same struggle, with its fortifying influences on character. And golf is good for the character in many ways. It is serious as life. It admits no peccadillos; it permits no compromises; it recognizes no venial sins. A false step, a scarce perceptible slip, — and you are lost. There is nothing to complain of in the conditions. The laws of the game are simple as the decalogue. Abstract and absolute justice is meted out to you. If you fail, it is you who are culpable and none other. But it is in this very simplicity and rigidity of law that there lies concealed, for aspiring and progressive man, the subtlest lure.

XXXIII

AFTER all, what leads you on in golf is this.
You think a perfect pitch of excellence can be
attained. But that pitch of excellence continually recedes the nearer you approach it.
Intellectual apprehension outruns physical
achievement. Accordingly, the allurement is
unceasing, and the fascination endless. Always you can imagine a longer drive, a more
accurate approach, a more certain put; never,
or rarely ever, do you effect all three at every
hole in the course. But all men — who are
golfers — always live in hopes of accomplish-
ing them. The conditions never vary; the
obstacles remain always the same; the thing
to be done to-day is precisely that which was
to be done yesterday, last year; and as man
never is, but always to be, blessed, as hope
springs eternal in the human breast, as progress, as development, is the one incontestable
instinct implanted in all things living, the

cosmic principle, the law of heaven and earth, the motive of all effort, the germ of all action —the phantom of perfect success flits ever before the ardent golfer. And what golfer ever was there who was not ardent?

XXXIV

How comes it about, then, that, if the conditions are so simple, success is so difficult? The fact is, there is enormous *chance* in golf. There must be, when you propel a cubic inch of gutta-percha over acres of soil. Were the links a gigantic billiard-table, chance might to a certain extent be eliminated, as no doubt in billiards it actually is. But the links being what they are, namely, some two or three square miles of open country, variegated in its every square inch, in any one square inch of which you may lie, and each square inch of which may affect differently the character of your stroke or the roll of your ball, chance, to

the beginner in golf, we may safely compute
as infinite. But, as one improves, the conditions being fixed and determined, skill di-
rectly eliminates chance. In no other game
is the equipoise between chance and skill so
exact, since in all other games a third and
variable factor enters into the problem, the
skill, namely, of your opponent. In nothing,
perhaps, is the perennial fascination of golf so
plainly to be found as in this direct ratio between the increment of skill and the corresponding decrement of chance. We may put
it thus : —

> Let a = skill, and
> Let x = chance ; then
> x varies from ∞ to 0 as
> a varies from 0 to ∞.

That is, when the skill is zero, chance is infinite ; when (if ever) skill is infinite, chance will
be zero. There is no likelihood of any links
losing their charm through the entire elimi-
nation of chance by reason of superlative skill.

Golf will never become a hazardous, outdoor billiards. It will take a million years to develope the muscular sense to such a pitch as that it will land the ball, after a hundred yards' flight, plumb on a given point, free from all cups, on a perfect lie—though, from the annually improving records for several links, the muscular sense is evidently tending that way.

XXXV

AND now, wherein lies the supreme mystery of this so-called "game"? In this surely, that whereas the thing to be done seems most easy of accomplishment, it is as a matter of physical and metaphysical fact a feat requiring the deftest use of the most delicate mechanism. Mind (or matter, which you will) in the long course of its evolution from amœba to man, has as yet, so far as we know, here upon this planet produced nothing more complex in structure than the human neural apparatus; and it is this apparatus, in its most secret recesses, that is called into requisition by every player at every stroke. And whereas the thing to be done is rigidly fixed, but the anatomical machinery by which it is to be done is capable, humanly speaking, of infinite improvement, the pitch of excellence at which we aim continually recedes the farther we advance, and we are lured on, and lured on . . . to the delight of professionals and caddies, to the pecuniary profit of club stewards and manufacturers of expensive balls, but to the sorrow of waiting wives and to the scorn of maledictory onlookers.

We can put no limit, humanly speaking, to the possibilities of the neural system. What the brain, the spinal cord, the nerves, and the muscles may not some day be capable of achieving, we cannot say; and to what pitch of perfection the associative memory may be trained it is equally impossible to determine. And every golfer feels in himself these

possibilities of improvement. Intellectual apprehension, I have said, outruns physical
achievement. Every golfer, that is, knows
precisely and definitely what it is he is called
upon to do; but he feels that the machinery
by which it is to be done may be indefinitely
improved — if only he can discover how to
improve it. Accordingly every golfer strenuously endeavours to improve it. "It can be
done; I can do it"; so every golfer says to
himself — he *will* do it, by the Styx he de-
clares he will. — The professional of my links
once went round in the magnificent score of
sixty-six. Upon my congratulating him, what
was his reply? "Well, sir, I missed three
puts. I can do it in sixty-three." Some day
he will,¹ and then no doubt he will say,
"Well, sir, I missed so-and-so. I can do it in
sixty-one." — Will he rest content then? Of
course not. And the same spirit urges on the
veriest duffer.

¹ I believe he has since done it in sixty-three.

[136]

The curious thing is that this extraordinary ambition seems to appertain solely to golf. On every round every golfer strains every nerve to break his own record. Nor is there any other game in which defeat is so poignantly felt. Why? We must fall back on the theory that it is because the thing to be done seems so simple, so patently, so palpably simple, that everybody thinks he ought to be able to do it, and *therefore* defeat rankles — rankles. Were it hugely difficult; did it require the superlative development of this, that, or the other intellectual or physical faculty, we should succumb with a good grace — as we do when we play with an acknowledged expert, say, of chess, or billiards, or whist, or whatnot. But in golf to succumb with a good grace is to acknowledge that in the very fibre and essence of the man who beats us there is something to which we cannot attain. — Which seems one more proof of the fact that in golf it is the very fibre and essence of a man that count; not mere power, or knack, or agility. And no doubt this is true. How many games have been won by indomitableness of spirit alone; how many by a quiet self-confidence; how many by a reserve and a restraint that can watch with perfect equanimity hole after hole won by unwonted brilliancy, and yet win by dogged and determined adhesion to steady play?

XXXVI

From all this is there anything practical to be learned? I am afraid not. If you have golfed from childhood, you will laugh at it; if you have taken up golf at forty, it will not be of much use to you. The youthful caddie, whose cortical centres are in a docile stage and who accordingly picks up the game by sheer imitation, and the elderly professional, who has done nothing but make clubs and swing them all his life, probably play almost automatically —as you or I wield a knife and fork, a spoon, or a pen. To the one, golf is what gambols are to the kitten; to the other, what mousing is to the cat. Not theirs to analyse the method of their play. I know a professional who says that in reality there is only one stroke in the game in which he has to keep in mind one little rule, namely, to play off the right foot in a hanging lie. How different from the amateur novice! I was playing the other day with a University professor, a charming man and an erudite. He happened to be off his drive, and at the fifteenth tee (a sequestered spot), with a sort of despairing cry to heaven, he muttered as he took his stance, "Now, I wonder whether I *can* for once keep my eye on the ball and follow through?" He did not even attempt to burthen his University brain with more than two, and these elementary, injunctions.

"But can you not tell us," I can readily understand the reader — by this time no doubt (and quite legitimately) impatient — saying,

" can you not tell us what it really is at bottom that wins in golf? What is the one thing needful? What is the pearl of great price? What is the great and important factor of success?"—My dear sir, would to heaven that I could! If I could tell myself, most gladly would I tell you.—However, upon one thing I presume all golfers will be agreed, upon this, namely: that, *all other things being equal* (but they never are), what wins is *dexterity*. Given two golfers absolutely evenly matched in character, temperament, and strength; both equally self-confident, collected, and careful; and victory will fall to the more dexterous. Other things being equal, if you can drive and approach and put as easily and effortlessly as a facile writer dots his *i*'s and crosses his *t*'s, you will win. There is no doubt about that. Golf is like writing with a crowbar. If Monsieur Paderewski could play golf as he plays Liszt's Sixth Rhapsodie Hongroise, nobody could beat

him; for in those rapid semi-demi-semiqua-
ver staccato octaves Paderewski combines a
strength with a dexterity marvellous to witness. But, curiously enough, in golf dexterity
seems to count even more than strength. I
have seen a superb little lady golfer, who assuredly could not have had more than nine-
teen birthdays, and who I am quite sure
tipped the scales well under nine stone, drive
ball after ball clean and straight, some just
under, some over, two-hundred yards—to
the delight and the admiration and the adora-
tion of great male golfers in the gallery. That
was due surely to the dexterity with which
she made use of all the strength she possessed.
At the moment when her club met her ball,
every ounce of weight and every foot-pound
of energy she could command were communicated to the ball, without altering by a hair's
breadth the even rhythm of her swing or the
faultless precision of her stance—nay, more,
she put her whole heart and soul into the

stroke as well; and these counted for much, very much. (If you wish to know for how much, I will tell you: at the eighth green I saw her pick up her opponent's ball, take a big piece of mud off it, and smilingly replace it. That showed the sportsman's heart and soul!) All I can say is, Go thou and do likewise. Ah! many were the grown men and women in that gallery who wished that they could!

Yes; I take it it is the consummate combination of strength and dexterity that — the psychological factors being eliminated — ultimately win. You may have the strength of an ox; but unless you have also the agility of a cat it will avail you little. Unless you can drive straight and judge distance to a nicety, mere length is nought. Yet on the other hand, unless you can cover a great deal of ground on your long game, even extreme accuracy on your short game is heavily handicapped. But the real and most effective combination is that of immense power with extreme delicacy. Therein lies the mystery of golf, so far as the mere bodily frame is concerned. It consists just in this, that you can wield a driver weighing a pound just as easily and as surely as you can a penholder weighing a drachm; that you can use your strongest muscles — almost every muscle in your body at once — at their extremest limit as easily and surely as you sign your name.—I am cock-sure my Pro can approach a hole better than he can sign his name. But, as we have seen, this effective combination of strength and skill is itself the result of some mysterious and inner psychic centres forever inscrutable to man.

XXXVII

JOHN STUART MILL once anxiously debated whether there would not come a time when all the tunes possible with the five tones and two semi-tones of the octave would be exhausted. So, many a non-golfing wife and unsympathising onlooker thinks there surely must come a time when the erring husband and friend will tire of trudging over the country trying to put half-crown balls into four-and-a-half-inch holes. The outsider does not know that at every hole is enacted every time a small but intensely interesting three-act drama.[1] There is Act I, the Drive, with its appropriate mise-en-scène: the gallery, the attendant caddies, the toss for the honour. At long holes it is a long act if we include the brassey shots. There is Act II, the Approach. This is what the French call the *nœud* of the plot: much depends on the Approach. And the mise-en-scène is correspondingly enhanced in interest: the lie, the hazard, the wind, the character of the ground — all become of increasing importance. There is Act III, the Put. It also has its back-ground, its ''busi-

[1] I gratefully acknowledge my indebtedness for the germ of this idea to a capital article by ''T. P.'' in *M. A. P.*

ness," and its "properties": the caddie at
the flag, the irregularities of the green, the
peculiarities of the turf, the possibilities of a
stymie.—Eighteen dramas, some tragical,
some farcical, in every round; and in every
round protagonist and deuteragonist constantly interchanging parts. No wonder the
ardent golfer does not tire of his links, any
more than the ardent musician tires of his
notes. What theatre-goer enjoys such plays?
And what staged plays have such a human
interest in them? And, best of all, they are
acted in the open air, amid delightful scenery,
with the assurance of healthy exercise and
pleasant companionship. What theatre-goer
enjoys such plays?—And when the curtain
is rung down and the eighteenth flag replaced,
instead of a cigar in a hansom, or a whisky-
and-soda at a crowded bar, or a snack at a
noisy grill-room, there is the amicable persi-
flage in the dressing-room or the long quiet
talk on the veranda.

[145]

Nor does the golfer ever tire of the stage upon which these his out-door dramas are played.—I have been promising myself time and again to go round some day, unarmed with clubs and carrying no balls, for the express purpose of seeing and enjoying in detail the beauties of my links. There are some woods fringing portions of the course most tempting to explore, woods in which I get glimpses of lovable things, and a wealth of colour which for its very loveliness I forgive for hiding my sliced ball. There are deep ravines—alack! I know them well—where, between lush grass edges trickles a tiny rill, by the quiet banks of which, but for the time-limit, I should loiter long. There is a great breezy hill, bespattered with humble plants, to traverse the broad back of which almost tempts to slice and to pull. A thick boscage, too, whereon the four seasons play a quartet on the theme of green, and every sun-lit day composes a symphony beautiful to behold.

And there are nooks, and corners, and knolls, and sloping lawns on which the elfish shadows dance. Smells too, curious smells, from noon-day pines, and evening mists, from turf, and fallen leaves. . . . What is it these things *say?* Whither do they beckon? What do they reveal? I seem to be listening to some cosmic obligato the while I play; a great and unheard melody swelling from the great heart of Nature.—Every golfer knows something of this. But, as Herodotus says, these be holy things whereof I speak not. *Favete linguis.*

XXXVIII

Lastly, let us not omit to include amongst the elements of the fascination which golf wields over its votaries that *gaudium certaminis*,[1] that joy of contest, which always the game evokes. It is one of the chief ingredients of the game,

[1] Thank you, W. H. B., for this hint.

and it is evoked and re-evoked at every point
of the game, from the initial drive to the ultimate put. It is an ingredient of every manly
sport is this "warrior's stern joy," but in
golf it is paramount and overt. Every stroke
arouses it, for the exact value of every stroke
is patent to both player and opponent. Few
other games keep the inborn masculine delight in sheer struggle at so high a pitch. No
wonder the stakes in golf are merely nominal;
no wonder that often there are no stakes at all;
the keenness of the rivalry is stimulus enough.
—And this, surely, is one of the chief beauties of the game. It will never be spoiled by the
intrusion of professionalism; at least it will
never be played by highly-paid professionals
for the delectation of a howling and betting
mob; nor, thank heavens, will rooters ever sit
on fences and screech at its results. At present
it is uncontaminated by either "bookies" or
"bleachers"; nay, it has not yet reached that
stage in its history when it asks for gate-money.

XXXIX

But the ultimate analysis of the mystery of golf is hopeless — as hopeless as the ultimate analysis of that of metaphysics or of that of the feminine heart. Fortunately the hopelessness as little troubles the golfer as it does the philosopher or the lover. The *summum bonum* of the philosopher, I suppose, is to evolve a nice little system of metaphysics of his own. The *summum bonum* of the lover is of course to get him a nice little feminine heart of his own. Well, the *summum bonum* of the golfer is to have a nice little private links of his own (and, now-a-days, perhaps, a private manufactory of rubber-cored balls into the bargain), and to be able to go round his private links daily, accompanied by a professional and a caddie. — It would be an interesting experiment to add to these a psychologist, a leech, a chirurgeon, a psychiater, an apothecary, and a parson.

XL

To sum up, then, in what does the secret of
golf lie? Not in one thing; but in many. And
in many so mysteriously conjoined, so incom-
prehensibly interwoven, as to baffle analysis.
The mind plays as large a part as the muscles;
and perhaps the moral nature as large a part
as the mind—though this would carry us
into regions deeper even than these depths of
psychology. Suffice it to say that all golfers
know that golf must be played seriously, earnestly; as seriously, as earnestly, as life.

XLI

But may not also the simple delights of the
game and its surroundings, with their effect
upon the mind and the emotions, be included
under the allurements and the mystery of
golf? My knowledge of links up to the present is limited, but on mine there are delights

which, to me a duffer, are like Pisgah sights:
hills, valleys, trees, a gleaming lake in the distance, a grand and beloved piece of bunting
lending gorgeous colour to the scene; a hos-
pitable club-house with spacious verandas
and arm-chairs; shower-baths; tea and toast;
whisky and soda; genial companionship; and
the ever-delectable pipe. Has anyone yet sung
these delights of the game? the comradeship
in sport, the friendliness, the community of
sentiment, the frankness of speech, the good-
will, the "generosity in trifles"? Or of the
links themselves? the great breeze that greets
you on the hill, the whiffs of air — pungent,
penetrating — that come through green things
growing, the hot smell of pines at noon, the
wet smell of fallen leaves in autumn, the damp
and heavy air of the valleys at eve, the lungs
full of oxygen, the sense of freedom on a great
expanse, the exhilaration, the vastness, the
buoyancy, the exaltation? . . . And how
beautiful the vacated links at dawn, when the

dew gleams untrodden beneath the pendant flags and the long shadows lie quiet on the green; when no caddie intrudes upon the still and silent lawns, and you stroll from hole to hole and drink in the beauties of a land to which you know you will be all too blind when the sun mounts high and you toss for the honour!

Afterword
by
John Updike

The text you have just perused, gentle golfing reader, is that of the first edition of The Mystery of Golf, *published in 1908 in a limited edition of only four hundred copies. The book's unexpected success prompted the publication two years later of a second, enthusiastically expanded edition, to which Arnold Haultain added a hundred additional pages of text, thickening the already rich texture of the prose with yet more quaint learning and fancy writing, with more foreign phrases, leisurely ruminations, metaphysical and physiological lore, and references to such worthies as St. Paul, Tennyson, and Yrjö Hirn. The editors of this series of golf classics have wisely decided to republish the earlier, shorter text, in which Haultain's few basic points are already more than sufficiently elaborated in the half-*

facetious, generously allusive style of turn-of-the-century essayistic writing.

We have here material for a solid short article finespun into a charming little book. Its core, however, is pure gold; with an analytical ardor that, as he says, only a tyro of mature years could have mustered (for the young beginner would not be so analytical, and the seasoned player not quite so ardent), Haultain goes to the heart of golf's peculiar lovability and enduring fascination. His shrewdest point comes early, in section V, and bears repeating:

> *... there is no other game in which these three fundamental factors— the physiological, the psychological, and the social or moral—are so ex- traordinarily* [the second edition substitutes the more telling adverb "intimately"] *combined or so con- stantly called into play.... In no other game that I know of is, first, the whole anatomical frame brought into such strenuous yet del- icate action at every stroke; or,*

second, does the mind play so important a part in governing the actions of the muscles; or, third, do the character and temperament of your opponent so powerfully affect you as they do in golf. To play well, these three factors in the game must be most accurately adjusted, and their accurate adjustment is as difficult as it is fascinating.

In no other sport, that is, does the player so continuously and closely have to perform as his own coach. "Every stroke," Haultain tells us, "must be played by the mind—gravely, quietly, deliberately." In no other sport are mental effort and concentration so immediately reflected in the mirror of physical action and its result. The tennis player crouched on the back line, the baseball pitcher on the mound certainly exhort themselves and inwardly rehearse some technical points; but they can also depend to a large degree upon natural ability and instilled reflex. Golf, it seems, must be learned afresh each time we tee off, and if on the one hand it humbles us with a sudden collapse of some aspect of play we thought had been mastered, it on the other always holds out, perhaps even more to the inept than to the expert, the hope of dramatic improvement. Haultain lucidly extols the fluid, multiform, neo-Platonic complexity of golf as a mental and—though his recurring emphasis on moral fibre as well as mental focus will strike us as old-fashioned—spiritual experience.

Those who can, do; and those who cannot, theorize. Out of his presumed embarrassments in practice Haultain developed a profound grasp of golf's lovely tensions. The chronic debate over whether the stroke is a swing or a hit is resolved in this sentence, worthy of memorization: "It is in fact a subtle combination of a swing and a hit; the 'hit' portion being deftly incorporated into the 'swing' portion just as the head of the club reaches the ball, yet without disturbing the regular rhythm of the motion." He troubles to express, too, the elegant paradox of the starkly simple objective toward which golf's many tools and advisements and way-ward incidents all tend: "to knock a ball into a hole—that seems the acme of ease." The late nineteenth-century's Darwinian obsessions sharpened Haultain's awareness of the elemental combat beneath golf's genteel for-malities—combat in which the human opponent is only the secondary enemy, the primary foe being "great Nature herself" in the guise of the course. He is an eloquent poet of the golf course, and his concluding paragraph is often quoted. Even more moving, to me, is his evocation, in section XXV, of the humble nine-hole course "far away on a western continent" (I took the con-tinent to be ours, and the course Cana-dian) where one throws one's coat over a fence rail and without further ado begins rapturously to play, over the hoof-marks and cart-ruts; for how many of us who love the game did that

*affection begin on such a modest, im-
perfect layout, whose grassless tees
and bumpy greens and cramped dog-
legs yet remain in the mind as the very
template of golfing bliss!*

*Haultain has proved not quite cor-
rect in his prophecy, in Section
XXXVIII, that golf "will never be
spoiled by professionalism; at least it
will never be played by highly-paid
professionals for the delectation of a
howling and betting mob." The mobs
do not howl, but they sigh and cheer,
and tournament courses have added
bleachers, and gate-money is part of
the deal. His sense of golf as an ex-
hilarating combat with an untamable
Nature might be dulled, I fear, by a
look at today's new courses, with their
watered and weedless fairways,
flowerbed-lined tees, and embank-
ments built of railroad ties. His confi-
dence, proclaimed in Section XXXIV,
that golf courses will never become bil-
liard tables and that chance will heal-
thily affect even the proficient player*

might be shaken by what bulldozers and sprinkler systems have imposed upon patches of the American wilderness. Modern rules, too, conspire against the genial mis-rule of chance. The average golfer will not accept a lie in a fairway divot any more than one on a sprinkler-head; and "winter rules" informally obtain even through the lushness of July. Haultain's tale of the chivalrous young lady who cleaned the mud off her opponent's ball on the green no longer makes much sense, since everyone now legally picks up and cleans his or her own ball on the green. Quite often one sees, on the televised tournaments, the ball marked and dusted for the second putt as well, which is carrying the war against chance to the microscopic level. Money and the masses—"'Arry and 'Arriet"— have certainly had their levelling effects upon the game of stalwart Man against rugged Nature that Haultain so exaltingly depicts.

Golf's innocent heart, however—the

lively tugging between the "motor" and "ideational" centers that takes place when we set ourselves, club in hands, over the ball—remains unchanged, along with the soaring flight of a well-struck shot and the welcome rattle of a purposefully executed putt. Haultain's introduction of the term "kinaesthesis" usefully suggests the portion of the sport that in the end must be relegated to "feel," to intuition of a deep physical kind, and also suggests the portion of our pleasure that relates to the un-parallelled (except in riflery) amounts of space with which a golfer must contend. The variety of strokes, from the forward-bounding drive to the back-ward-skipping sand wedge, plus all the improvised punches and cuts that our mortal straying forces upon us, composes one of the game's inexhaustible charms. But Haultain says it best:

> *In golf you get the whole gamut of the muscular sense, from the gigantic swipe at the tee to the gentle tap*

on the green. It is called into play at every stroke, and it differs with every difference of club—its weight, its length of shaft, the angle which its face subtends to the horizon, its rigidity or flexibility, the construction and material of its head.—Golf, in short, is a sort of Gargantuan jugglery, a prodigious prestidigitation, a Titanic thimble-rigging, a mighty legerdemain.

For all its sober, relentless numerical aspect, golf affords the player magical sensations, under the skies, amid the infinities of space and chance, and this its curious central ecstacy has never been more thoughtfully addressed than here. It occurs to me to add that this "Gargantuan jugglery," whose stresses so comically break us into multiple personalities (Section XX), in sum creates for each devoted player a separate self, his golfing self, who waits for him at the first tee when he has put aside the personalities of breadwinner and lover, father and son. This release into another self, surely, is not the least beguilement of the mystery.